D1107963

AND
ANOTHER THING...

By HOWARD SPRING

HARPER & BROTHERS PUBLISHERS
NEW YORK AND LONDON

In Memoriam

WILLIAM HENRY SPRING

DIED AT SEA

BURTON SPRING

KILLED AT ARRAS

4-6

FIRST EDITION

C-V

AND ANOTHER THING . . .

WHAT an unaccountable thing human memory is! It is stuffed with unrelated odds and ends, matters of no significance or value, and these will not depart to make room for all the great moments, the vital experiences, as we choose to consider them, that we would gladly remember.

A phrase came into my head this morning : "Though it was November, a few leaves still hung on the trees." How far back does this take me? I don't know; for here is another queer thing about memory : even in what it chooses to retain, it is partial and selective. The phrase was written by an author named Maclaren Cobban. Not many people, even while he lived, heard of Maclaren Cobban. I can tell you the name of only one of his books : *The White Caid of the Atlas*. That was a romantic yarn for boys, and I read it when I was very young. Maclaren Cobban also wrote "thrillers", and the phrase I have quoted occurred in one of them. This, too, I must have read when I was very young, but here capricious memory withholds everything save the phrase itself. The title of the book is gone; so are the circumstances of the reading; so is most of the book's theme. It is a sad reflection on the efforts of us authors that a novel may be read and leave no more trace than this : one phrase, and that unremarkable. Why it has stuck in memory who can say? Perhaps at the

time it was read it echoed a personal experience that had
been sharp and clear.

It is all absurdly unimportant, but I try to clarify it. I
can get as far as this. When I was a messenger-boy employed by the *South Wales Daily News* in Cardiff, there
was a row of tin boxes fastened to a wall of the room I
worked in. On each box was the name of a member of the
staff. In the morning I would go down to the "front
office", collect the letters that had come by the first post,
and distribute these into their boxes. Only one of the
boxes interested me, and that was the one belonging to the
editor of the *Cardiff Times*. The *Cardiff Times* was our
weekly edition ; it contained a serial story and other " mag-
azine " matter. Moreover, the editor of the *Cardiff Times*
selected the short story which appeared in the first column
of the back page in our four-page pale primrose evening
paper, the *South Wales Echo*. Furthermore, anything of a
" literary " nature that came to the office went to the box
of the editor of the *Cardiff Times*, and under the word
" literary " was included with a fine generosity such publi-
cations as *Chums* and certain others that, for whatever
reason, were sent to the office weekly. There came, too,
from a firm in Bolton, which specialised in " syndicating "
cheap fiction, galley proofs of novels that the *Cardiff Times*
might use as serial stories ; and so, what with one thing and
another, the *Cardiff Times* editor's box was always stuffed
with what seemed to me matter of import and significance.
For, from my childhood, fiction and the people who wrote it

2

had for me an allure, almost an enchantment, that was, for whatever reason, the deepest feeling of my life at that time; and this feeling had no reference to the nature or quality of the thing written. I had not, then, any equipment for deciding about such matters as nature and quality. It was enough for a man to have written any work of fiction : I was his liegeman.

How catholic this devotion was a few illustrations will show. The editor of the *Cardiff Times* in those days was S. C. Fox, who at this time of writing is still, at a great age, a working journalist in my native city. As my own years roll away, I realize more and more clearly how much my opening mind owed to the ever-present but never obtrusive influence of this dear friend. It was he who, whenever I won book-prizes (as I had a habit of doing) for work in evening classes, chose the books, and chose (as I now see) with a perfect discernment of what was necessary for me at the time. It was he who lent me Forster's *Life of Dickens,* and I recall how, night after night, I would retire to a not-usually occupied room in our little house, light a lamp on the table, prop up a picture of Dickens under the lamp, and read the Master's life. It was an act of devotion ; but, as I have said, my devotion was vapid and diffuse where writers of novels were concerned.

Among all that heterogeneous stuff dropping into the *Cardiff Times* box there came every week a paper called *The Young Man,* and the serial story in it was being written by the editor, who was a nonconformist parson. My

3

joy was great, my agitation extreme, when a bill on a hoarding announced that this man was to preach some sermons at a chapel in our city. That a novelist should appear in a pulpit, where the common people, including myself, might hear his voice and look upon his face, seemed to me a happening within the realms of the miraculous. I can recall the fearful expectancy with which I walked across our city, literally from one end to the other, to hear that sermon; but, alas! of the sermon itself, of the appearance of the man who delivered it, not a trace remains. Even his name has slipped through the holes in memory's colander.

It must have been at about this same time that Cardiff fell victim to that measles of "pageants" that was spotting the country everywhere. The book of our local show was written by a novelist named Owen Rhoscomyl. I believe his real name was Vaughan. But books—authentic books, with his name on the title-page and stiff cardboard covers —had been published, and that was enough for me. One day when I was at work in the room that contained all the little tin boxes a stocky, clean-shaven, blue-chinned man came in and asked to see the chief sub-editor. I enquired his name, and he answered "Owen Rhoscomyl". If he had said he was the Grand Cham or the Tyrant of Tartary he could not more completely have flabbergasted me. This was the first novelist with whom the gods had permitted me to exchange words. I conducted him through the short corridor that led to the sub-editors' room, and John Smurth- waite, I wager, never guessed the awe with which I announced this visitor. "Good day, sir. Take a chair," he said ; and that at least seemed to me fit and proper. Owen Rhoscomyl should be called "Sir" and he should at once be offered a chair, seeing that no throne was available.

It all, now, at times seems childish, green and immature, this obsession with writers, no matter what they wrote ; but at other times it seems right and proper, a necessary and fortunate phase, and I can be glad that I was not born into circumstances in which everyone and everything was taken for granted, but into a humble place where stars, of however small magnitude, yet were stars, meet for worship and wonder.

Mr. Maclaren Cobban and his phrase which started me on these random wanderings have been left behind, and we must get back to them : back to the tin box of the editor of the *Cardiff Times* in those days of forty and more years ago. S. C. Fox never discouraged my rummaging in the contents of the box, and many were the serials in galley proof that I read from among those sent along by the Bolton firm. It surely must have been there that I came upon this story by Mr. Cobban. Of the story itself, the name is gone from me and I can recall but one incident. It was a crime story, and there was a problem in it : namely, how did the criminal perform some remarkable " get-aways " ? (Oh, memory, memory ! The very name of the story has suddenly flashed up out of this deliberately disturbed sediment of my mind. It was called *The Terror by Night*.) The incident that I recall is that the criminal per-

5

formed his remarkable deeds by wearing on hands and feet clever suction contraptions that permitted him to move about on walls, or for that matter on ceilings, like a fly !

And now we've come to an end of this experiment in turning over the insignificant *trivia* of memory. We arrive at an unimportant writer named Maclaren Cobban, a book called *The Terror by Night,* an idiotic episode, and one complete phrase : "Though it was November, a few leaves still hung on the trees."

*   *   *

It is November now. Last night was full moon, and we had a fine 17 feet 9 inches tide in the roads. The night came on cold, and I had that slight ache in the bones which always tells me there is frost about. As I slept I could yet hear the cats leaping one by one through the bedroom window. There are six of them at the moment, but they don't all come into the bedroom. Their sybaritism varies in degree. Some of them leap on to the hot-water tank in the kitchen. Clothes are usually lying there to air, and they settle down on them like the moujiks over the stove in a Russian story. But some prefer the bedroom, moving round a bit in the night, now in the armchair, now on my wife's bed, now on mine. They are jealously possessive creatures. "What I have I hold" is their motto. Recently a neighbour went for a holiday and we took in Randolph, one of our kittens which we had given to her, as a boarder.

6

There was no peace in the house at all. His own mother wouldn't look at him. His brother considered him an interloper and snarled at every sight of him. All over the place were feline nerves obviously on edge. Kittens that grow up into the family are one thing : they slowly make their way into the community and are fully accepted ; immigrants, even those returning to their homeland, are another matter : they are shown unmistakably that they are not wanted. As soon as Randolph went home tempers simmered down, and now we are a peaceful household again.

At half-past eight, which would be half-past seven by Greenwich Mean Time, I went into the garden, and it was then that that phrase of Maclaren Cobban's stirred in memory and came to the surface. For, though it was November, the trees were thick with leaves. It was a morning of great beauty. To the west, the white exhausted-looking disc of the full moon still hung high above the horizon, behind the screen of elms, eucalyptus and pine. To the east, across the water, the sky over St. Just was full of ruddy light. A milky smoke was rising from the quiet sea : quiet save for faint ripples which, as they stirred, brought out a pattern of pale blue undulating smears among the whiteness. The elms were in their full panoply of gold, all except the immense widespreading elm which reaches from the lawn furthest out over the water. He is half bare. Always, for some reason, his leaves are the first to go. He is a noble tree, with his roots anchored down into and far beneath the lawn, his branches reaching out over the water and then drooping, so that in high summer a majestic umbrella of green shade is spread there. A gangway from the lawn goes out into the heart of the tree, and on a hot June day you can sit there in the cool of millions of leaves, looking down to the water beneath you, enclosed by the drooping ends of the elm branches like water in a cave. Sometimes the wild swans come and dally there, and then the enchantment of the scene is perfect.

This morning, despite the sharp sniff of frost in the air, it is difficult to believe that this is November. The frost has not been enough to spoil the dahlias whose great heads of red and white are still perfect under the north wall of the house. The chrysanthemums are in full beauty, too, blooming in every colour, and the Michaelmas daisies will be with us a long time yet. So will the fuchsia hedge that is in full flower. And when all these are gone, and the elms are really bare, even then, here in this sheltered bit of southern Cornwall, we shall not lack flowers. The primroses are the glory of our earliest spring. It is difficult to think of any colour, or any shade of colour, in which they do not abundantly bloom. Already they have begun. With industry, hunting in this part of the garden and that, I could assemble a good bunch ; and at least a dozen long-stemmed violets are filling the air with fragrance. The buds are thick on rhododendron and camellia, and the grey-green feathery leaves of the mimosa are already a background for the tenderest hint of the flowers that will be

8

upon them, fluffy and yellow as day-old chicks, before we know where we are.

These are agreeable things to notice as I make my way to the rocky bank where the thyme grows. Some is wanted for the kitchen. But the light frost has robbed the thyme of all its perfume. I squeeze it and pinch it, but never a whiff of odour comes from it. So I try again down by the pond where the little leaden boy for ever stands wrestling with his goose, glistening with the sheen of the water falling from the fountain. The pond is a dead-looking place to-day. The sun has not yet touched it. The reeds have drooped and snapped, folding their points into the water, and the water lilies that were such glories of red and cream and white have contracted into nodules of brown corrupt-looking matter, slowly sinking beneath the surface. The goldfish and rudd that flash electrically through the summer water are dull and sluggish. But down here there is thyme that the frost has not reached. I squeeze it, and smell. It makes me think of baked midsummer rocks on the moors of the West Riding.

*　　　　*　　　　*

The pigeons are as bad as the cats in their possessive greed. Nothing could be fairer to look at. They are white fantails, and to see them tumbling through the air against the blue sky is a joy. The wooing sound that ceaselessly bubbles from the male throat is honeyed and soothing. I

9

could listen to it for ever, as to the sound of the water
falling into the pond from the alabaster basin of the fountain. I have known people driven almost mad by this endless crooling of the pigeons, but it helps to tease out the
tangles of my mind and keep it quiet. It is so with all
natural sounds. When I am in town, living in a hotel, I
get little sleep. The honking of motor-horns, the shrill
whistles of porters calling taxis, the grind of trams along the
Embankment, the gurgling of the water as someone next
door decides that 1 a.m. is a good moment for bath and
song : all these things make the city night a horror. But
here the herons often tear the night with that harsh appalling cry that makes me think of winged monsters hunting
through primeval swamps, and the plaintive lovely calling
of the curlews goes on at all hours. These, with the crying
of owls, are our characteristic night sounds, and they have
no power to disturb me. They are half-heard in sleep and
seem only to emphasize the peace of the night over the
sea. In the daytime the magpies add their chatter and the
jays their raucous assertive shouts, but they all tune in to
the orchestration of nature and leave the mind at ease.
What, considered dispassionately, could be more discordant
than the cawing of rooks ? Yet it is the very sweet of the
day in early spring as the busy dusky birds clot their nests
into the leafless pattern of the elms. And there are so
many sounds that have enchantment in their own right.
The twittering chorus of the turn-stones is one of them.
Always of an evening, when I walk along the beach before

getting in to work, I come upon them hunting their microscopic prey among the seaweed edging the tide. They allow you to come within a few yards but, though all the time they are in busy movement, you do not see them till, in marvellous unison, they rise and skim away over the water, very close to it, fifty or so in a bunch, turning and twisting as if with one will, and filling the air with a sharp, vital, twittering call. Then, perhaps thirty or forty yards away, they will drop down again to the undulating weed, and instantly they are lost to you once more.

It is easy to imagine, watching the healthful flocks of birds enjoying the liberty of the air, that all is peace and happiness with them. I remember coming off a Home Guard patrol with a townsman who was living in our parts and a countryman born and bred. It was mid-summer, and across the roads the sky was rosy with a perfect dawn. The townsman looked about him like a boy on holiday. " I feel as happy as a bird ! " he exclaimed. The countryman replied briefly : " Birds are not happy."

In the tall Douglas fir at the top of the garden the gold-crested wrens have their nests. They are tiny things, the nearest we have, I suppose, to a humming-bird, and they flash like dynamic thistle-down through the air, preying upon gnats. I have held one in my hand, but it was dead, a cat's victim. Unbelievable that this thing whose weight was literally imperceptible had been such a vital spark of beauty. But happy ? Hardly, I imagine. The gold-crested wrens are harried as unmercifully by the jays and magpies as peaceful shepherds were by the Vikings. In the nesting-season the inaccessible recesses of the Douglas fir—inaccessible to me—are clamourous with the loud cries of the hunting birds. The jays, beautiful butchers, take a heavy toll, and seem to delight in screaming as they massacre. They have the offensive spirit so beloved of those infantry instructors who teach recruits to utter blood-curdling yells as they tear out the straw entrails of sacks with their bayonets. Perhaps H. F. Lyte was right in hymning the

> Happy birds that sing and fly
> Round Thy altars, O Most High,

but our common garden trees are not altars and see much slaughter.

Apart from the slaughter of bird by bird, there are tragedies enough to be witnessed. Coming shorewards in the dinghy this summer, I saw a black-backed gull standing on the beach, and wondered that he did not make off when the boat grounded. When I had tied up, I walked towards him, and he retreated, keeping always ten or a dozen yards away. Evidently he could not fly, but I could not see the reason. He went away from me with a hopping run, sometimes stretching out his wings on either side, so that evidently they were not broken. Nor could I see any trace of the oil that dooms so many seabirds with its cloying embrace. His legs, too, were perfect, and there was no sign of a wound on him. When I stood he would stand, and so from a short distance I was able to observe him.

Normally, there is a cold and cruel arrogance in the staring eye and predatory beak of a black-backed gull. But if you can imagine a bully who for some reasons has had all his bullying knocked suddenly out of him, and is moreover manifestly sick to death, then you can imagine how the gull looked. With nothing wrong that the eye could discern, there was obviously everything wrong. This gull had the unmistakable look of death about it. The air and the sea were its elements, but it could not take to the air, and once or twice, having advanced to the sea's edge, it entered the water only because of my approach, and rocked on the tide a few feet from the shore without spirit or enjoyment. As soon as I withdrew, it came back to land, and stood without movement looking over the sea that once had been its kingdom, its bed and its larder.

I went into the house and brought some tit-bits that I thought might tempt it to eat. How eagerly, and with what vivid cries in happier days, when we had been lunching on the cutter, the gulls would wheel around screaming for odds and ends, their great wings flashing ! But there was no flash in this gull. It edged away from the food I threw as from missiles ; and then there was nothing else to be done. I left him there.

Late that night I came down to the beach to see if the gull were still about. The spring tide was at full, so that there was no beach any longer. The water washed right up to the granite wall that guards the lawn from erosion. On top of the wall is a thick hedge, and under the roots

13

of the bushes the gull was crouched, looking down into the water. There was something infinitely sad in the beauty of the midsummer night, and the water, that could be so furious, lapping peacefully against the grey granite wall, and the bird that was the incarnation of freedom upon air and water huddled there, denied by some mysterious doom the enjoyment of his heritage.

All the next day the gull was there—a pale lifeless spectre of a gull—painfully moving to and fro between the steps from the lawn at one end of the wall and the boathouse at the other. To this small terrestrial beat was doomed the creature of sky and sea, whose companions were leaning upon the wind and with no movement that the eye could see climbing and diving in all the hills and hollows of the firmament. A bird in a cage always sickens me, and I was sickened by the sight of this king of birds dying in a cage that had been invisibly set about it. As the tide made that day, and again that night, it feebly retreated from its own element and shuddered under the shrubs that housed the wrens and tits. And in the morning it was gone, but I never knew what was its end. Certainly, so sick it was, it never again took to the sea with its webs or to the air with its wings. But somehow it had vanished from the earth to which it never belonged.

*   *   *

I accused the pigeons of possessive greed. Looking at their beauty on a summer's day, no one can wonder that artists put sprigs of foliage in their beaks and make them symbols of peace. But my bachelor would not consent to this opinion. There are three of these white fantails : father and mother and their bachelor son. Once the bachelor had a brother or sister—I don't know which ; but a cluster of feathers on the lawn was all that remained one day of this fourth member of the family. A cat, no doubt.

I had cut a hole through the garage wall, high up, and inside this was as pleasant a home as pigeon could desire. It was a happy home, too, when the bachelor was young. He grew into a handsome youth, as fine-looking as his father, and soon as big. It was then that the trouble started. One evening I noticed that the bachelor was on the step outside the hole that leads into the cote and that he was exchanging by no means loving pecks with his father, who was within. Clearly he wanted to get to bed ; and no less clearly his father was resolved that the time had come for him to sleep elsewhere. They would have been biting one another had they been capable of biting ; as it was, they were exchanging furious pecks. The warfare persisted day and night. There could, at last, be no doubt about it : though this cote could comfortably house a score of pigeons, it was destined to house no more than two. An Oedipus complex in the columbarium was something I had not bargained for, but the matter had to be dealt with. I could not punch holes all over the garage wall in order to make homes within ; so to the outside of the wall, near father's front door, I fixed a box with one side open. It was only just big enough for a pigeon to get into,

15

and I am always promising myself to make something more commodious. But it serves well enough. A house-agent would call it a "bijou one-roomed flat", and the bachelor retires to it at night happily enough. But the *casus belli* is always present, and amicably though this trio flies through the air and feeds on the lawn, ever and anon there is a battle on the parental doorstep. Not once have I seen the bachelor regain his old home since the day when he was thrust forth.

Meanwhile, the lady produces eggs with a regularity which I should like the hens to copy. Now what am I to do about this ? If I allow the eggs to hatch, either I shall have a succession of scandalous episodes or I shall have to plaster bachelor apartments over the garage front as thickly as swallows' nests under the eaves. I solve the matter by removing the eggs. Beaten up in a little warm milk, they make excellent pick-me-ups for *enceinte* cats, of whom there are always a few about the place.

*   *   *

The astonishing fertility of the cats is something the eugenists and students of "vital statistics" should admire. Our Lucy and Malinskaya must surely be to them models of feminine thought for the future. Lucy is maternity pure and simple. She is a big tortoiseshell who lives to have kittens and to suckle them with sensuous joy. When they are big enough to be weaned, she becomes a hunter, ranging the garden in search of field mice, and, as she approaches the house with one dangling loosely beneath her whiskers, she utters a call that the kittens at once know to mean "Hey! Meat!" Out they run as soon as that sound is heard; and, leaving them to it, Lucy will hoist herself on to the hot-water tank in the kitchen and loll there in fat content, her yellowish eyes withdrawn upon some dream of the next batch of young.

If Lucy is all maternity, Malinskaya is all femininity. She has as many kittens as Lucy, but she never forgets that she is a woman first and a mother afterwards. She is an enchanting grey creature who has never allowed her body to acquire Lucy's look of needing corsets. Between her pregnancies she thinks a lot about her figure, and to see her dancing on the lawn on a summer night is to understand why she has been given a name out of ballet. In fact, she is doing nothing more than pursue shadows and leap after gnats and flies. But what lovely leapings and rapturous pursuits! For most of the time she is reserved with us, "stand-offish" enough, but when she gives herself over to courting us, what feminine wiles, what shameless coquetry and cajoling! She will lie upon her back on your knee, reaching up her white gloves to stroke you, her eyes of indescribable green swooning under a film of sentimental moisture that she can wash over them at will. I often think : God help the Tomcat that Malinskaya has set her heart upon. When her kittens arrive, she mothers them well, but not with the stolid mammalian emphasis of Lucy.

17

She makes one think of a society woman to whom the children are brought in by a nanny, while there she is, waiting perhaps a little impatiently in her grey fur coat, ready enough to give the children their due, but aware that life has other interests.

But, with all their differences, each is a prodigal mother. Our friend Doctor Doolittle, who delighted the infancy of my sons, was able to learn the language of any animal. If he could be induced to extract from Lucy and Malinskaya the bones of a lecture on careless happy maternity and deliver it up and down the country, this would greatly please those who are in a blue funk about the declining fertility of us Britons. Students of such matters have been telling us for a long time that we are heading for a stupendous drop in population, and the situation is serious enough to have at last attracted attention in the highest quarters. Yesterday's *Daily Telegraph* begins a paragraph "By our Political Correspondent" with a piece of queer mathematics. "Every married couple," the paragraph reads, "should have two children, or preferably three, to maintain the population of Britain. This is the main conclusion of a report, 'Tomorrow's Children', published to-day by the Tory Reform Committee."

I'm afraid the Tory Reform Committee will have to go a bit deeper than that. The phrase "or preferably three" suggests that, with two children to each married couple, this business of maintaining the population could just be carried out, and that three would make it certain. But this

18

is not so. A married couple is two people, and, if they have two children, they have, so to put it, one child each. Which is to say one reproduces one, and therefore the population does not increase but remains constant if . . .

Yes, there is an " if " in it. There are indeed several " ifs " in it. If all the children born are neatly arranged into exactly one boy for exactly one girl. Otherwise where are your matings ? If every child born remains in the land of its birth. If every child born lives to maturity. If every pair born marries. If death, which has obligingly consented to be banished thus far, agrees farther to hold his hand until every one of those marriages has produced two children. Only in these conditions, which are not improbable but impossible, could the population be maintained by each married couple having two children. If each married couple had three children, something would be done to offset the effects of death before maturity, of emigration, of failure to marry and sterility after marriage. But even so, it seems to me the situation would still be chancy. The population *might* be precariously maintained if—and this matter is full of " ifs "—war passed us by ; but, even granted all this, three children out of every marriage is hardly likely to result in an *expanding* population. I should say that to make certain of the population remaining stationary, and to give it a *tendency* to increase rather than decrease, it would be necessary for four children to come of every marriage ; and how far we are from this being the condition of affairs we know too well.

There are those who thoughtlessly say : " What does it matter, anyway ? A small population can be as happy and prosperous as a big one." In the condition in which the world now finds itself, and in the condition towards which the world is clearly moving at an accelerated pace, this is not true. Despite all the talk of all the conferences and conclaves that are assembling here and there, this is still, and will for a long time remain, a highly competitive world. In this competition, our part is primarily that of an industrial people. To " keep our end up ", to maintain our industries in an efficient condition, demands the existence of great armies of workers. From this point of view a heavy drop in the population would be disastrous. It is, of course, not the only point of view. Those who speak of a small and happy breed of men, existing in communities mainly agricultural, reviving the crafts, and not even disdaining the use of machines for a necessary minimum of purposes : these would view without dismay the disappearance of the industrial towns of Lancashire and the West Riding, the Potteries and the " Black Country ", the Clyde and the Hartlepools ; but before arriving at dogmatic conclusions on these matters it would be as well to consider the convulsive agony that this adjustment would require, the stupendous problems of the artisan millions who could not be supported in this small land in the conditions which this set of thinkers envisage. In any case, the inevitable destination of our present line of march can only be an intensification of life as we knew it before the war, with one increasing

20

difference. This is what I call the condition towards which the world is moving at an accelerated pace, and I mean that we shall see a great growth in the charity state. Beveridge Reports, Government White Papers, and what not, are nothing but the inevitable response to a demand that is too deep and widespread to be ignored. Increasingly, the State has levied its toll on life and treasure. "If blood be the price of Admiralty, Lord God we ha' paid in full", and the demand grows that the State that asks much shall give much. If the inevitability of our direction is towards a condition in which the industrial population must continue, then that vast and hungry Demos will know its own power sufficiently to wring out of the State its fair share of what it contributes to the State.

And so the words "charity state" which I have used are not the right words, but Demos, though he is learning, has yet to learn fully. He has to learn *ex nigilo nihil*, and that he can get out of the State only what he puts into it. His sound case at the moment is that, thus far, he has not got even this. If it can be proved that there is not enough to go round, well and good; but at least it must also be proved that what there is is going round.

Now where all this links on to the population problem which Malinskaya has brought to our notice is here. You can't run a state saddled with enormous grants, pensions and other services on a falling birth-rate. The Tory Reform Committee puts it briefly : "Beveridge and all the rest will be so much moonshine with a declining population and always more coming on the pension-list and fewer to the plow, the tractor and the lathe."

My father used to recite to me this tag :

> The world has two sorts of fellows, I ween,
> The fellows who lift and the fellows who lean.

In a Beveridge state, I suppose the fellows will begin to lean utterly round about the age of sixty-five. If the birth-rate continues to fall, we shall gradually acquire more and more of these leaning fellows and fewer and fewer at the lifting end, until at last the burden becomes too heavy for the lifters and the whole business collapses in ruin. This end would be the more quickly reached because State-granted medical service, and so forth, would tend to preserve and prolong life, and a growing congestion of hearty octogenarians would clog the hive like drones fed by an ever-decreasing number of worker bees. It would not be an unnatural consequence if, then, the charity bee-state took one more lesson from the custom of the hive and the workers, in a sudden fury, solved their problem by falling on the drones and killing them off. They would at last have learned the lesson that the amount of honey which can be got out of a hive is precisely the amount that is put into it. And putting it in means work; gruelling and continuous.

It will be pointed out that this analogy is imperfect, indeed utterly misleading, for we shall be dealing not with drones but with superannuated workers. But the conse-

22

quences to the economy of the workers will be the same, no matter what the past history of those they have to support. That the augmenting regiments of old people are morally entitled to be kept will not do a thing towards solving the physical problem of keeping them.

*   *   *

So what are we to do about it, since the charity state is inevitable, since it cannot be long maintained on a falling birth-rate, and since the birth-rate is falling ? The Tory Reform Committee " recognises in all humility that the foundations of the desire for parenthood and the innermost aspects of fertility are beyond the knowledge and control of politicians as such". Well, thank God for that, anyway ! And thank God, too, that a committee of politicians recognises something " in humility". This is a new note in this world of plans, schemes, white papers, blue books, with which politicians, civil servants, and novelists dizzy us, yelling their fool-proof outlines of heaven on earth.

But, since a committee must suggest something, this committee suggests family allowances, labour-saving houses, crèches, cheap maternity homes, almost everything except giving babies away with a pound of tea. Well, let's try anything, but I for one, though I too have some humility in face of this most complicated and mysterious problem, do not expect much to follow from making the physical conditions of life easier. Experience does not give encourage-

23

ment in that direction. And what experience have I to go on ? Primarily, my own and that of my parents. My father was a day labourer in gardens. Throughout his married life, my mother has told me, he brought into the house about a pound a week. There was no family allowance. The house was not "labour-saving". It had no electricity, or even gas. Cooking was done in an antiquated kitchen range that had not even an oven, so that a joint, when there was one, was kept spinning on a string; lighting was by oil-lamps and candles. There was no bathroom and no hot water save what was boiled on the fire. There was no "domestic help for mother", such as this kindly committee suggests. Indeed, my mother was busy rendering domestic help in other houses while her children were about her. There were no "crèches and nurseries, cheaper maternity homes with private wards". An old local "grannie", not widely removed from the standards of Sairey Gamp, was the midwife. There were no "privileges for parents, such as priority for new houses, travelling and entertainments". Entertainments ! I cannot remember my mother going to an "entertainment" throughout the whole time of the raising of the family. She had nine children. Here, you would say, is an encouraging example of fertility, for has not the Tory Reform Committee told us that "two, or preferably three" children would keep things straight ? And here are thrice times three. What happened to the nine ? Two died in infancy. Four girls and three boys grew to maturity. Not one of the girls married, and two

24

are now dead. Of the three boys, one died of tuberculosis in early manhood ; one was killed in Arras in 1917 ; I alone survive. I have two sons.

Now my married life was a different matter. Without going into detail, I may say that I was able to provide all the things which this committee proposes that the charity state should give to parents. Yet the consequence of my parents' marriage was nine children ; the consequence of mine was two. And that is why I am sceptical about soft lives producing large families. So far as I am concerned, the whole matter is not a problem that can be solved but a mystery which we do not understand.

One thing is certain, and that is that, though this is a devilish world, it is, in the intervals between its wars, and for millions of western people, a more prosperous world in physical things than it has ever been before. Mr. R. F. Harrod, who early this year published a pamphlet called *Britain's Future Population*, points out that for centuries horror, war and pestilence have not daunted man in re-producing his kind ; but that this factor of growing pros-perity is a new thing. It is possible, he suggests, that prosperity and anxiety go hand-in-hand. This anxiety, and the widespread use of efficient contraceptives, are his two guesses at the cause of what he calls a "major crisis" and "no ordinary vicissitude" in human affairs. But they are only guesses ; he admits that.

*　　　　　*　　　　　*

The views of a lot of young women concerning this question of marriage and children have been getting into the press, and what I find disturbing is the general demand for a life without difficulty. I look back over fifty-six years, and it seems to me that the yeast in the bread of life and the savour in its wine have come out of the rough-and-tumble, the unpredictable, the addressing of oneself year-in-year-out to the demands of each day, each hour, as it arose. Before this book is published I shall have enjoyed twenty-five years of marriage, and how flat and barren those years could have been had they not been diversified by difficulty and enlivened by a multitude of small problems encountered and overcome! Among the happiest moments to which I and my wife look back are the very moments which these young people are crying out to be spared. They ask : "How can we get out together and know one another if there's no one to look after the babies?" The question turns back the reel of memory to some of our most golden hours. Shall they ever be forgotten, those Manchester days when the whole family set forth as a caravan ? I commend a perambulator as a hold-all for a day afield. What things we packed into it ! The babies and the babies' bottles, our own food, our books for reading in the sun, thermos flasks and a change of napkins ! We would be away all day, pushing the pram out from Manchester into the Cheshire lanes and by-ways, and getting to know one another better thus than if we had handed the children over to a neighbour and betaken ourselves to dog-track or cinema. There

26

are places we shall never forget : one field in particular
where no one seemed ever to come, and the hedges in June
were full of meadowsweet and foxgloves. There we would
lie for hours against the bank, and eat our food, and spread
out the blanket for the younger baby to kick on while the
elder wandered through his elysium of cuckoo flowers and
buttercups.

Or we would push the laden pram to the nearest rail-
way-station, put it and the dog into the guards' van, and
go far afield, alighting in some Cheshire paradise where
lunch could be eaten by a stream of sweet water and tea
bought in a cottage garden. These are memories we would
not exchange for any state-provided "universal aunts",
taking off our hands a responsibility that was a joy. As
life goes on, I think the proving of love is not so much in
enjoying together, though there is also that, but, more
fundamentally, in enduring together, just as true comrade-
ship arises from the battle, not from the spit and polish, or
the carefree pints in the canteen ; and a life in which a
smooth official hand removes all that calls for endurance is
likely to be one in which the strongest links that bind men
and women together are smoothed away too. They may be
found too weak to hold when stress comes, as come it will
in any estate, however regulated. Enjoyment may provide
the chromium plate, but it is the things endured together
that provide the bolts and rivets. As for the night out now
and then, there must be something wrong with people who
cannot find a neighbour willing to stand into the small

27

breach. To have a good neighbour, you must be one ; and good neighbourliness depends on good character, which in turn depends on all those imponderables that are born out of the small difficulties of life, welcomed and overcome. God help us if we seek to be nothing but trams running on smooth municipal rails.

* * *

There has been of late some correspondence in the *Daily Telegraph* about Field-Marshal Rommel. He had been praised by a writer in that newspaper, and this displeased many people. One letter to the editor damns Rommel outright as a gangster—" a criminal who perished while trying to escape from the police ", a man who " condoned the crimes of his employers ". A little later in the letter comes an important phrase, and all its implications had better be explored : " There is a real danger to mankind in this tendency to relieve the professional sailor, soldier or airman of the normal dictates of conscience or of the proper exercise of free will."

I do not see why the adjective " professional " is used here. Are we to have a free-willed staff commanding armies of robots ? I shall leave the adjective out, and consider this important question : "Can free will be allowed to a soldier, sailor or airman ? "

Before we go any farther, let us be sure that we are not deceiving ourselves, that we mean what we are saying, and

28

that when we ask soldiers to follow the dictates of conscience, we grant this permission to our own soldiers as well as to those of our enemies.

At the time when this discussion about Rommel was proceeding in the *Daily Telegraph* an interesting thing was happening elsewhere. The British had invested a town and called upon the commander of the German forces who held it to surrender. The German commander refused to do so, and the British artillery was thereupon ordered to blow the place to pieces. It housed many civilians, and a British officer had scruples of conscience about blowing civilians to pieces. He therefore refused to carry out orders and was placed under arrest. Later he was sentenced to a year's imprisonment.

I saw no letter in the *Daily Telegraph* or elsewhere protesting against this treatment of an officer who was doing what the denouncer of Rommel suggested that an officer should do : that is, obeying the dictates of conscience and exercising his free will ; and this did not surprise me, for the truth is, or so it seems to me, that a soldier can *not* be allowed to follow the dictates of his conscience or to exercise his free will.

There are two reasons for this, and they hang together. The first is that mankind is in a low state of moral development. I remember walking, some time before this war began, through the streets of London with a well-known writer who suddenly began to shake with laughter. I asked what amused him, and he said : "I was thinking

29

what a lark it's going to be when the people of this country realise that they are *not* living under a democracy." My companion was an ardent Catholic, and I could have replied that it would also be a lark when people realised that they were not living in Christendom, but I did not do so because neither the one discovery nor the other struck me as having the elements of amusement.

Yet it is a fact, if Christendom means a territory subject to the laws of Christ, that we do not live in any such kingdom. We need a simplification in our view of what that kingdom is. For two thousand years the teaching of Jesus has been overlaid with such accretions of theology, so decorated with pomp and ceremony, that the simple digestible bread of it has become as garish as a Christmas cake. It is time the world, for its own safety and sanity, realised that behind mitre and triple tiara and all the other spectacular gimcrackery of a world organization there is a simple man walking our common dust in sandals, and talking a divinity so humane that the wayfaring man, though a fool, may not err therein.

The divine humanity and human divinity that Jesus taught was no more than that God is love, and that the proof that a man had made this great discovery, had entered into the love of God, was that he in turn loved those about him. The greater part of the teaching of Jesus was concerned simply with this : the ways in which, *here below*, this love which came from entering into the universal love of God could manifest itself in love of the brethren.

30

The disciples and apostles in their turn emphasised this as the core of the teaching. It is the constant undertone of the First Epistle General of St. John : " He that loveth his brother abideth in the light. . . . For this is the message which ye heard from the beginning, that we should love one another. . . . He that loveth not abideth in death. . . . Beloved, let us love one another : for love is of God : and everyone that loveth is begotten of God and knoweth God. . . . If a man say, I love God, and hateth his brother, he is a liar : for he that loveth not his brother whom he hath seen cannot love God whom he hath not seen."

We have Paul's memorable conclusion : " The greatest of these is love ", and the essence of love, he went on to explain, is that it forgets all those things that come under the heading of " self-interest ". It " seeketh not its own ". So far from going out after the things of another, it holds its own things to be of no final account.

This was a correct interpretation of the teaching of Jesus, for he again and again insisted that the self and the things of self were what stood between men and their absorption into the love of God. He would go to all lengths in the denial of self in order to avoid conflict. There is no getting beyond the record on which Christendom claims to be based. If a man wanted your coat, you should give him your cloak, too ; if he smote one cheek, you should turn the other. " Ye have heard that it was said, Thou shalt love thy neighbour and hate thine enemy : but I say unto you, Love your enemies."

How far, in two thousand years of Christendom, have we come towards making this teaching the basis of conduct ? And it is not as though during all that time the Christian churches had had to fight for survival. Throughout centuries the power of the state, and if not the enlightened support at any rate the consent of the greater part of the people, have been with the church. And we have come to where we are.

And where have we come to ? Again let us go to the newspapers, a useful mirror of our times. A London vicar appealed for comforts for German prisoners. An Ipswich vicar contributed a tin of rat poison. Now this vicar, I take it, at his ordination was asked by his bishop : " Will you be diligent to frame and fashion yourself and your family according to the Doctrine of Christ, and to make both yourself and them, as much as in you lieth, wholesome examples and patterns to the flock of Christ ? " And again I take it, he replied : " I will apply myself thereto, the Lord being my helper."

And, fashioning himself " according to the Doctrine of Christ ", we have this outburst of bizarre humour. On the one hand the example : " Father, forgive them, for they know not what they do." On the other, the modern fashioning : a tin of rat poison.

The Bishop of Ipswich reproved the vicar, and no doubt it would be easy to make too much of what was, to put on it the most charitable interpretation, an upsurge of Old Adam. But we must note that nine hundred soldiers sent

32

a deputation to thank the Ipswich vicar for what he had done, and he told a reporter : "Nearly 300 letters from every part of the country have poured through my letter-box." No doubt when 300 letters pour through the letter-box of a Christian vicar the teaching of one mis-guided carpenter flies out of the window; and we may further be sure that the 900 soldiers and the 300 letter-writers were representative of thousands of citizens of " Christendom ".

What does all this lead us to ? To the wry laughter with which we contemplate the " lark " it will be when men wake up and realise that, after two thousand years of Christian teaching, " Christendom ", with its monuments weltering in ruin from one end of Europe to another, is a word to make cynics smile and angels weep. Whether " Christendom " cares to face the fact or not, Jesus was a pacifist and would have had no part or lot in this bloody shambles which besets us. I have not kept the reference, but I remember that William Temple, the late Arch-bishop of Canterbury, publicly declared that a Christian might with a clear conscience take part in the war. That may have been the sincere view of William Temple, for whose opinions on the whole I had a deep regard ; but there is no getting beyond the fact that this was not the view of Jesus. I see no logic in an attitude which on the one hand insists that Jesus was not man but " very God of very God ", whose word was literally the voice of God speaking in the world, and on the other tells us that a follower of this omnipotent and omniscient and all-wise God may with a clear conscience act in flat contradiction to God's teaching on a vital matter.

My own view is that the teaching of Jesus is beyond the moral grasp of man as he is, and that, in the world as it is, man cannot live by it. I see that I myself have fallen into a common delusion and spoken of the simplicity of his teaching; it is usual to hear that expression : " That is all the teaching is, fundamentally : Just love one another." But the truth is that this " simple " command asks of us something which makes the most subtle and complex of philosophies look like A B C. To love one another, as Jesus understood the words, demands a life of such self-sacrifice—literally the sacrifice of self, every bit of it—such utter death to our personal strivings and ambitions, such a profound understanding of the need of others, and such psychic skill in placing our all at the service of others, that the average human, dominated as he is by greed and fear, has as much chance of entering fully into this condition as a Stone Age man would have of making an aeroplane. The potentiality may be there; it is a man, even as that ancient being was a man, who at last will make the aeroplane, but his own contemporary way of life cannot be influenced by this fact, though imagination may allow us to conceive here and there among these primitive people one or two vaguely visited by dreams of what man might some time do.

No one can look round Christendom to-day without

34

realising that men, after two thousand years of the teaching of Jesus, are as near to making it manifest in their lives as those Stone Age men were to flying among the stars.

It is significant that, although Christendom is founded upon the conception of God which was brought into the world by Jesus, it is not to Jesus that the martial Christian appeals. Nelson's last words were not " Jesus and my country " but " God and my country "; and Cromwell did not urge his troops to " Trust in Jesus and keep your powder dry ". He, more than most others, would have seen the incongruity of that. There are occasions when we unconsciously slip back two thousand years to the pre-Jesus view of God : the view that he himself examined and put aside. " It has been said by them of old times . . . But I say unto you . . ."

There would be some happiness if we could reflect that men were at any rate making an advance towards enlightenment, but the evidence that they are doing anything of the sort is hard to find. When, within one generation, the world has twice quivered beneath so ghastly a shock as that which we now experience, and when the second outburst has revealed not a diminution but an extension of the human appetite for death, then one may be excused for seeing the world as a fruit with a spreading rottenness at heart that threatens the collapse of the fair appearance. There would be some hope if, beyond this present shovelling of victims into the jaws of Moloch, we saw the certainty of peace. But peace to man can come only on the terms that Jesus laid down. In this world of planning it is overlooked that the plan was given us two thousand years ago. There can be no peace save where love is ; and love has not notably increased of late in the human breast. So it is without surprise, with little more than a fatalistic acceptance of doom, that we listen to declarations that "Germany is already preparing the next war", and that we ourselves, in order to deal with this fact, must prepare even more fearful engines of destruction than we already possess.

You will never get rid of war by declaring in an international congress that it is "outlawed". War, like everything else, must exist in the mind before it can come to the deed ; and an idea can only be thrust out of the mind by the coming in of an idea more powerful. The fundamental idea that gives rise to war is the fear idea. The bully is notoriously a coward, and the bully nations are dominated by fears : fear that their pride, their prestige and what not is touched, fear that they are not getting their share of the world's loot, fear of the intentions of their neighbours. "Perfect love casteth out fear."

Even the horror of war would contain a germ of consolation if wars were waged for the establishment of righteousness. But as each race "awakens" and looks about it in the world, it is attracted by the fatal glitter of wealth, ease and mechanical contrivance ; and there is no more nobility in the modern power struggle than in a beggar's coveting of a Rolls-Royce and the fur-coated

36

woman lolling on its cushions. For this Japan blows up
the East; and there are other races yet to come upon
"awakening": black and brown and yellow races, num-
bering countless millions, who in the fulness of time will
become as expert as we are in the not exacting business
of pressing buttons and turning screws that detonate
charges of high explosive. Is it to be wondered at if the
Western nations, the nations of Christendom, by their
frenzied hanging-on to their material possessions, by their
determination that the rest of the world shall have them
only as buyers, only as contributors to industrial profit,
give to these things in the eyes of "awakening" nations a
sense of value which material contrivances in fact do not
and never can possess? Has Christendom any higher
value than this to suggest as desirable to the peoples of the
East? Is industrial efficiency all we have to offer? Mr.
Alaric Jacob, in his book *A Traveller's War*, writes of
India : "The Japanese are helping. Thanks to them,
factories are working overtime, industrialisation grows
apace and the Indian Air Force advertises : 'Wanted—
Men who can Plan and Command. Nationality Indian
or Anglo-Indian', and offers wages and a way of life profoundly glamorous to young India. The war is opening
up careers and opportunities never known in peace and,
even if the political stalemate continues, with elected
governments functioning in only five provinces out of
eleven, India will come out of the war far stronger indus-
trially and more independent commercially than she
entered it."

In a phrase of great candour but disturbing implication, Mr. Jacob asks of Indians who follow Gandhi : "Don't they realise that to win freedom in the modern world a Lenin, not a saint, is what they need ? "

So the time for saints is ended, and the shape of the future begins to loom out of the mist : an emergence from this present struggle of new "great powers", who have shown no signs of being different from the old "great powers", possessive, arrogant in material might ; and, behind and beyond these, the as yet "unawakened" people who, as surely as day follows night, will "awaken" in their turn into a world unredeeemed by love.

We begin, while the present war still roars about us, to be reminded of our part in this world to come. Admiral Sir William James has drawn, for the delectation of a Primrose League meeting, what a newspaper calls "a rather Wellsian" picture of future war. The pilotless bomber, said Sir William, "does cause one to scratch one's head". He added : "There can be no doubt that if the scientists of the world bend their minds to the problem, the flying bomb will steadily increase its power and become more and more accurate."

A few days later Sir Miles Thomas, the vice-chairman of the Nuffield organisation, gave us a few more words on this same subject. The range of these bombs, he said, can now be developed "to an undreamed-of degree". (Why undreamed of ? Someone seems to have had this consoling dream.) These monsters hurtling through the air, with "homing devices" attached (that is, addressed more

specifically than before to your home and mine) might
" well decide the outcome of future wars ".

So monster begets monster, and the " bigger and more
beautiful bombs ", over which we were called on to re-
joice, come home to roost, bringing their tails behind
them. "The outbreak of the next war," Sir Miles Thomas
said for our cheer, " may well be heralded by silent, invisible convoys of aerial missiles coming from great dis-
tances under the guidance of radar beams."

In the same paper which contained this report of Sir
Miles Thomas's speech, Mr. Arthur Oakeshott, Reuter's
special correspondent, reported on the affray off the bloody
beaches of Walcheren, where out of every five little ships
four were lost : "As I watched from my landing craft
close inshore, ship after ship burst into flames and disappeared in a pall of smoke and flame or blew to pieces
with a terrific crumbling roar, or again yawed helplessly,
engines smashed, steering gear gone, and the crew and
cargo of Commando tanks and equipment virtually anni-
hilated. Many a landing craft drifted past me with bodies
strewn over the decks and bridge, and other parts of the
ship showing great gaping holes where shells had passed
through, leaving death and destruction in their wake."

Man, incapable of making a blade of grass, can do all
this, and for the future he can begin already to dream of
bigger and better bombs, having the advantage of being
more carefully addressed to the right places. This was the
day when I was in Plymouth. In a gaping hole beneath
a ruin two children were playing at housekeeping. They

had bits of shattered slate for plates and saucers, and
flowers in a jam-pot decorated their table of splintered
plank. Bills were posted here and there about the town,
inviting the citizens to hear Professor Abercrombie speak
on the New Plymouth. I could have cried in savage
scorn : " Back to your catacombs, troglodytes ! Why
waste your substance on a New Plymouth when a simple
' homing device ' may have your home in its address book ?
Why bother with architects when the scientists have you
so thoughtfully in mind ? Have you never heard : ' Except the Lord build the house, they labour in vain that
build it. Except the Lord keep the city, the watchman
waketh but in vain ' ? "

But there was no place for savage laughter in Plymouth.
There was place for tears, and, watching the children with
their wild flowers beautifying the cave in the ruins, there
was room for reverence before the unconquerable spirit of
man. Whatever there may be of shaping moral purpose
in the world, I thought, these two children are nearer to it
than the devisers of " scientific development " and " freedom " by industrialisation in whom so many would have
up put our trust. In all the rest of Plymouth the Son of
God would have found little but cause for tears ; here,
perchance, he might have found the refreshment of a smile.

*   *   *

I know it is no doctrine of the Christian Church that
mankind is in a state of grace. Rather, against Words-

worth's theory that we come "trailing clouds of glory from God who is our home ", it sets the doctrine of original sin. The experience of mankind suggests that this doctrine, repulsive as it is to the self-esteem of many, is based in truth. Man unregenerate does not get far, and mankind to-day is as far from regeneration as it was two thousand years ago. My complaint against the Church is not that its general philosophic view of mankind is too severe, but that its day-to-day attitude towards the conduct of men in the world is not severe enough. I shall not here consider the leniency and complacency of the Church's attitude towards men in many of their daily activities which the teaching of Jesus does not excuse ; I speak only of this question of war because it seems to me that, in no circumstances whatever, can the warrant of Jesus be found for a Christian's participation in it. Yet, strangely enough, it is precisely in time of war that the Christian Churches awaken to a more than customary activity, associating themselves to the hilt with the national cause. It is interesting and significant that in Russia, where the divorce between Church and State was deeper than in any country in which Christianity had made its influence felt, the movement towards an understanding between the two took momentum in wartime. And, indeed, it is not difficult to understand that in a time when thousands must die and inflict death, the Church's sanction of the manner of their death and killing will be an asset of enormous value to the state.

In Russia this sanction could hardly be more generously accorded. The Orthodox Church there has not only called upon Christians all over the world to join in the extermination of Fascism but also "condemns those who call for mercy in the name of forgiveness". This is reported in a message from the British United Press and Exchange, recorded in the newspapers of February 7th, 1945. It is worth noting these facts with some particularity, for, even amid the craziness of the modern world, this is the first time, so far as I know, that a large section of the Christian Church has clearly stigmatised mercy and forgiveness as properties to be condemned. We have moved a long way from the God whose property is always to show mercy, and from forgiveness unto seventy times seven. I am not at the moment asking whether this attitude is necessary to man in the condition to which he has reduced himself. I am simply pointing out that here we have a church officially promulgating a view which could not be more profoundly different from that which the founder of the church advanced as the only one that could bring man into accord with the will and purpose of his heavenly Father ; and again, I ask : " Are we living in Christendom ? "

*   *   *

The early editions of Hobbes's *Leviathan* have a picture showing the head of the State grasping a sword in one hand and a crozier in the other. Antoine de Riverol, the

eighteenth-century French epigrammatist, whom I know
only from a few extracts in Bridges' *Spirit of Man*, has
commented upon this alliance of state and church in a
brief profound passage :

> Que l'historie vous rapelle que partout ou il y a mélange
> de réligion et de barbarie, c'est toujours la réligion qui
> triomphe ; mais que partout ou il y a mélange de barbarie
> et de philosophie, c'est la barbarie qui l'emportent . . .
> En un mot, la philosophie divise les hommes par les opi-
> nions, la réligion les unit dans les mêmes principes ; il y a
> donc un contrat éternal entre la politique et la réligion.
> Tout état, si j'ose le dire, est un vaisseau mystérieux qui a ses
> ancres dans le ciel.

I translate thus : " Let history remind you that wherever religion and barbarism mingle, it is always religion
that triumphs ; but that wherever barbarism and philosophy mingle, it is barbarism that carries the day. . . .
In a word, philosophy divides men through their opinions,
religion unites them in mutually-accepted principles; thus
there is an eternal contract between politics and religion.
Every State, if I may dare to put it so, is a mysterious
ship whose anchors are in the heavens."

Nevertheless, it remains my conviction that, so far from
pronouncing it permissible for a Christian to engage in
warfare, a time of war is the time above all others when
the Church should make it clear that, in the view of Jesus,
a Christian should do nothing of the sort. There are few
who would take any notice of what the Church had to say

in this matter. Diminishing in number as the Church's professed adherents now are, they would probably diminish at an even greater pace if the Church should take this stand ; but we should then know who were Christians and who were not. The Church would discover that its first function was not to enlarge but to purify its membership, for the cause of true religion is advanced not by churches becoming full of men but by men becoming full of God. We should see that such boastful hymns as Baring Gould's assuring us that " Like a mighty army moves the Church of God ", could not well be farther from the truth. The truth is that the Church of God, a different thing from the membership roll of any Church, has in all times been a pitifully small remnant of mankind, a tragically wavering light in a world of darkness. It has been a torch, passed from hand to hand, in generation after generation, faintly shining through vast landscapes peopled by the shadow of death. It has little to do with enthusiastic crowds, gathered in popular music-halls, and indulging in orgies of nationalistic sentiment watered with religious phrases. The few who accepted the full implication of the teaching of Jesus would realise that, in the present state of man's development, as far removed from " Christendom " as a candle is from the sun, they are not likely to set the world ablaze, and are therefore under the deeper compulsion to guard in its absolute and original purity the only flame that may at last do so.

For the present state of man's development is such that

Christianity is of no use to him, if by Christianity we mean not what the Christian Church consents to and endorses but what Jesus taught. This is the only conclusion I can come to as I consider the state of the world to-day. Perhaps some day a condition will exist from which men of a truly Christian civilisation will look back upon us with the tolerant wonder that we ourselves direct upon the struggles of troglodytes and Stone Age men; but, for the time being, we are what we are, and must do what we must do, accepting a doom which is not the less inevitable because our own folly contributes so heavily to its weight. In the tragic texture of our destiny the sins of our fathers are the warp and our own follies the woof; and the dark fabric thus contrived is shot through here and there with the bright embroidery of noble deeds and splendid aspirations. That is as far as man has arrived. It is not a Christian condition, but it constitutes the social and mental environment which compels much of his action, willy nilly.

This condition, this mental environment, of which I speak can be profitably studied in a book called *Why We Lost Singapore*, by Dorothy Crisp. This author's view is not that man's moral progress must necessarily be slow but that the mere idea of moral progress is " ludicrous ".

" We Lost Singapore ", she writes, " because we failed to remember that but two things are constant in this world : the facts of human nature and the facts of geography. Instead, we adopted the ludicrous Victorian theory of moral progress and decided that the world would

45

be pretty-pretty for evermore. We forsook Christianity without having the guts to forsake religion altogether, and arrived at the ridiculous point of pouring adulation upon certain by-products of Christian belief while ceasing to possess any vital spark of faith in the Christian God. Thus we became mere humanitarians."

This is a paragraph containing much truth and much error. In my view, Miss Crisp is right in charging us with having forsaken Christianity "without having the guts to forsake religion altogether". What we have done is to forsake the New Testament and fall back on the Old Testament's darkest conception of a tribal god whom we adore so long as his preoccupation is to bring success to the military enterprises of his chosen people. Miss Crisp should be the last to complain about this, for such a conception of God is the only one possible to a mind which accepts, as she puts it, "the essential and eternal brutality of life".

She has no right to chide us for "ceasing to possess any vital spark of faith in the Christian God", for we *must* cease to possess it if we are to live in the way she desires. The Christian God is God as interpreted by Jesus, and Jesus for one thing did not believe that "the facts of human nature" precluded moral progress. He was, I imagine, at least as well equipped as Miss Crisp to understand the facts of human nature, and his understanding of them led him to think that within those facts was comprised the possibility of change for the better. As he put

46

it, a man could be " born again ". A basic point in his teaching was that, as the relation of man with God is personal and individual like the relationship of a son with his father, and not comprehensive and amorphous like the relationship of a nation with its leader (which is why religious mass-emotion is to be distrusted), an advance of godliness in the world will come from the changed individual affecting the whole (within the limit of his potentiality) rather than from some general vague intention of the whole to benefit individuals. The Victorian " humanists ", at whom so many stones are hurled to-day by those whose own passion for righteousness is more limited than theirs, misunderstood, I think, the essential nature of this distinction. This misunderstanding led them to express their faith in that right thing " moral progress " in a wrong way. They believed that society could save individuals, whereas the truth is that individuals must save society. They got hold of both the cart and the horse, but they put them the wrong way round ; and that makes them no worse than their detractors to-day, who have neither cart, horse, nor road to travel on.

Another score on which Miss Crisp chides the English people is that they do not live up to their reputation for reading the Bible. She gives us the verse : " What king, as he goeth to encounter another king in war, will not sit down first and take counsel whether he is able with ten thousand to meet him that cometh against him with twenty thousand ? " This, to Miss Crisp, is an example of " the simple and effective practicality of the Four Gospels ", and she wishes we had borne counsels of this sort in mind when considering the defense of our empire. However, we don't need Jesus to tell us that, other things being equal, a big army will probably beat a little one ; and in the brief years of his ministry he had too much to do to waste his time on uttering platitudes for their own sake. Knowing the appeal of platitudes to the average mind, he liked to use them to illuminate spiritual truth ; and if Miss Crisp would care to examine what he was talking about, instead of abstracting an illustration from the context of the matter illustrated, she would find that the point here is that the Kingdom of God has no use for half-measures. What Jesus is saying is that this Kingdom, whose basic law is love and a belief in moral progress—that is, in the approachability of man to God—demands everything a man has. He must turn away, if necessary, from his own family. He must " bear his own cross and come after me ". Well, then, he goes on, using the platitude to drive the point home, you see that this means something tremendous. It's a warfare. Don't be like a foolish king who goes to war without knowing what he's going to meet. Consider the cost well, because you're taking on a big enemy, and " whosoever he be of you that renounceth not all that he hath, he cannot be my disciple ". From Miss Crisp, one would imagine that Jesus was talking about the material strength of armaments. Those who know something of his teaching will hardly be surprised to find that, in fact,

48

he was talking about the spiritual strength of renunciation.

While I join with Miss Crisp in wishing that people would read the Bible, I wish further that they would not pluck off a rose here and there, to illustrate, like Yorkists and Lancastrians, their self-interested devotion to one side of a battle. There is a " simple and effective practicality " of roots and thorns in this teaching : roots that go a bit deeper than military armaments, thorns that compose the crown of those who will bear the cross and " come after me ". That a writer can, within a few pages, dismiss the idea of moral progress as " ludicrous " and chide us for not hearkening to the words of Jesus, is the perfect illustration of the chaos into which we have fallen.

*　　　　*　　　　*

Now a further circumstance of man's present condition in the universe is this ; and it is a circumstance of primary importance : that such moral development as has taken place has been unevenly spread. It needs no chauvinistic nonsense—it is a matter of simple observation—to determine that at this moment of time the British, French and American people are in a state of higher moral development than the German people. We have all been guilty of follies and crimes enough, but, looking at the dark fabric of humanity, one sees some bright threads of nobility on our part of the map ; and on the German part a clot of appalling blackness unrelieved. Detesting as I do that

49

unreasoning frame of mind which cries "My country, right or wrong", I am almost grateful to the contemporary German for his enormity, because now there need be no unreason : evidence for the most cautious mind has been by these barbarians lavished tragically thick upon the blood-soaked, pain-tortured fields of Europe. "Atrocity" has been brought back, by a conscious and widely accepted act of will, as a means of human government : atrocity built up into a thousand shapes of ingenuity, so that there is no question of accident, but an almost stupefying plenitude of evidence that we are confronted by a conspiracy to employ human pain, intensified and prolonged, for the furtherance of a political end.

It seems to me that human baseness can sink no lower than this. If my memory serves me aright, Storm Jameson has said in one of her books that she cannot conceive of any mental torture that is worse than physical pain, and this is a view I share. The Nazis know well that the mental torture they inflict on those whose dear ones they seize as hostages is itself founded in dread of the physical pain the hostages may suffer ; and our mental agonising about those who are separated from us by the circumstances of this epic and brutal time is compounded of images of what they may be called upon physically to endure. Only a god, or men of godlike stature, can suffer real agony of soul from the contemplation of folly and sin.

So awful to me is the thought of physical suffering consciously inflicted that recently it intruded into my dreams, carrying me to a landscape of terrifying immensity. I stood on the edge of the sea and before me lay a great fish. All around, and as far as the eye could see, were strange red pulsating forms, an infinity, a universe of them. It seemed then as though the fish had appeared in its wholeness only for a moment in order to let me see that it was a living thing, for even as I watched it, strips of the flesh mysteriously disappeared until it was carved down, like all these other things about me, to a creature that had been deliberately cut to the point where, while still alive, all its nerves would feel the greatest impact of pain. Then I was aware that all the things I was looking at were animals and huge fishes palpitating with a rhythm of anguish. Stretching back and back, they were formally arranged in a pattern of platoons and companies, all a wet ghastly red, and the shapes in which they had been cut were stylised and attractive. Indeed, over the whole scene, and this was part of its horror, there was a strange surrealist beauty. There was not a sound anywhere, but the pulsing movement, which I knew to be pain, throbbed and surged, as regularly as a piston's beat, through the whole host, and beyond them the earth itself had shrugged up into corrugations that were undulating with this same identical beat of pain.

It was the most horrible dream I have ever had, because I was so aware of the beauty as well as the loathsomeness of the scene. I think I was close to an apprehension of the bestial sadism that has become an instrument of gov-

51

ernment. Then I saw that at my feet a huge bird was lying, of eagle shape but with the head of a tortoise. This was not mutilated like all else within view. It was perfect in form, but something had injured it, and it lay with its wings stretched out to their magnificent length along the ground, feebly moving its head. In the inconsequent way of dreams, I found then that one of my sons was suddenly at my side and that we were near our home. We ran into our cellar, and I seized an axe and gave him a baulk of wood. Then we rushed back to where the eagle lay, still alive and looking with its horn-hooded tortoise eyes at a group of people who had assembled. Some were shouting " Kill it ! " but one man was saying that it was his and that nothing must be done that would spoil the skin. "Where would my profit be ? " he demanded. In a white passion I shouted " Blast your bloody profit," and told my son to put the block under the bird's neck. He did so, and with a blow I severed the head from the body. And at that moment, all along the beach, all through the corrugations of the tortured earth, the ghastly throbbing ceased. Death had been allowed quietly to take its own.

A strange thing about this experience was that it was dream and not nightmare. From a nightmare I awake at the moment of crisis, sweating and frightened ; but this experience was absorbed into the sequence of sleep. At the moment when the pulse of the world's pain ceased, sleep came quietly to me.

*　　　　*　　　　*

For myself, I can frame no more terrible indictment of a people than to say that this dream formalised all my thinking about what the Germans have done to the world. The appalling thing is that we are left no longer in the realm of surmise, suspicion and conjecture : a majestic and terrifying amplitude of evidence now shows us with what manner of people we have to deal. And it is equally evidential that the civilised nations have morally advanced to a point where such diabolism is, for them, not only improbable but impossible.

The situation which had arisen, then, as I see it, was one in which this diabolic tribe, armed to the teeth, was ready and anxious to strike down the peoples who had advanced, to a conception of living which, however far from perfect, was an immeasurable step in advance of anything the Germans had shown themselves capable of understanding or even of faintly apprehending. Leaving aside for the moment all that could be said about our own contributory weakness, fear and folly, that was the situation. What was to be done about it ? If the words of Jesus mean what they say—and if they do not, I for one give up the struggle to understand where we are—the Christian could take no part in the attempt to kill as many thousands of these people as possible. For that is what war is : not to love your enemy but to kill him ; not to turn the other cheek but to cut off his head ; not to give him your cloak when his menaces demand your coat but to say : " No ; come forward another yard and I'll cut you to pieces."

53

Now it is my view that this is where we must not shilly-shally and try to show that the words of Jesus meant one thing when they said another. This is where we must say that, the situation of the world being what it is, and men being what they are, the words of Jesus are of no use to the situation in which we find ourselves. To have literally obeyed the commands of Jesus would have been to allow a bestial form of government to overcome such shy and tentative advances to righteousness as we have made, for, whatever may be its consequences in the long run, non-resistance to evil, as we have seen with painfully naked eyesight in this modern world, does not turn evil aside in that short run with which we have to concern ourselves. Rather it gives it the wherewithal to glory and drink deep.

The pacifist, which is what a true follower of Jesus must ever be, has tended in all times to expect the impossible. He has tended to expect immediate consequences from his pacifism. One of George Fox's celebrated letters to Oliver Cromwell makes it clear that Fox believed that if Cromwell sheathed the sword all his enemies would at once lie down and peace inhabit the world. This does not appear to have been the belief of Jesus. He deprecated the use of force not because he thought by that course immediately to disarm the wielders of force and to make them impotent, but because he believed that to use physical force in any circumstances was wrong. Those who disagree with me will point to the one occasion on their side of the argument : the occasion when he drove the money-

changers from the Temple; but for myself I am not prepared to allow one action, performed suddenly in the heat
of a passionate moment, to outweigh the whole course
and tenor of the teaching. No; I do not think Jesus expected non-resistance to overcome the immediate evil.
Thus, when Peter drew his sword and vigorously defended
his Master from those who would take him, Jesus said,
"Put up the sword," not because his non-resistance would
prevent his arrest, for he knew that the arrest and all its
consequences were before him, and he accepted that.
"Put up the sword into the sheath : the cup which the
Father hath given me, shall I not drink it ? "

To bring this whole matter to a conclusion : that, as
I see it, is the true attitude of the follower of Jesus—to
accept pacifism *and all its dire immediate consequences*,
not expecting an immediate miracle, but knowing the outcome of this struggle *sub specie aeternitatis*. Most of us
are not equipped with the moral grandeur that makes this
attitude possible. Rightly or wrongly, setting aside the
teaching of Jesus, we cry in very human appealing ac-
cents : "To do a great right do a little wrong, and curb
this cruel devil of his will."

*　　　*　　　*

I have written thus much in an endeavour to crystallise
my own views, and I find that they have worked out to a
paradoxical conclusion : that the Church should stand

unflinchingly by the absolute purity of the pacifist teaching of Jesus; that if it does so, few men will now follow it; and that if it does not, it will be betraying the command to love which is the only reason for its existence and the only hope of keeping alive that nucleus of divine fire to which, in the long run, man must return or perish. For my own personal part, the paradox is even profounder, for, while I could have nothing to do with a Church that was not pacifist, neither, in the present state of man's moral being, could I dissociate myself from the physical struggle in which his own imperfections involve him. For, concerning that struggle, there is this to be said : that, the world being what it is, it constitutes the buffer state, itself in continual agitation, behind which the pacifist is permitted to move towards his eternal objectives.

The pacifist often does not recognize this side of the matter. Though he is, in my opinion, in the right on the long view, he is, as a rule, far from the being that Jesus would have considered a good disciple. For one thing, he is too often merely a negative objector to the deeds of others, not a constructive worker for the world's good. To ask permission to be relieved of the consequences of men's follies is not the finest contribution to human advancement, and I sometimes wonder how many pacifists would say " Put up the sword " if they realised that the upshot of this would be their own immediate and painful death. Yet only such pacifism as that has any final significance ; only such pacifists as those are

men of Jesus, lovers of mankind; and that is why the
light of true religion, which is true love, shines through
so pitiful a chink in the world's darkness. For not many
such men are born in any generation. Certainly, they
have never made a "mighty army". They have never
been enough to lighten the world, but they have never
been too few to keep a lighthouse beam shining upon
the welter in which distracted man surges up and down
the dark undulations of his fate. Most pacifists, alas, are
as imperfect as the rest of men, and even such good as
they have attained could easily be swept away but for
the interposition of that buffer state of fighting men. I
think it is incontestible that the German foulness was
within measurable distance of overwhelming Europe. I
face the fact that the command of Jesus is that we should
lift no physical hand against our enemies; and I ask myself
what would have been the consequences had we obeyed
that command? My own view is that such light as there
is in Europe would have been dimmed almost to extinction, if not quite. I think the only answer the Christian
can make to this is that somehow, in God's good time, His
will would have been worked and the kingdom of non-
aggressive, co-operative, loving men would have come to
the world. This God's-eye view, with all eternity for its
perspective, is the view of the true man of Jesus. It is a
view that does not strive nor cry; it believes that the
Kingdom of God cometh not by observation; a thousand
ages in its sight are but an evening gone; and it knows

57

with a sublime assurance that man's home is in the love of God. But, eternally and indestructibly right as this view is, the average man *cannot*, in this present moment of time, live by it. He sees it as the lighthouse gleam across the midnight water; but his own task is amid the heaving waves and the darkness, within the narrow compass of the vessel that is his little life. .

*   *   *

The ways of God are too patient for men. We prefer to fight for a thing rather than to wait for it. "Be still, and know that I am God" is an intolerable command to most of us. Be still! Few of us can find five minutes a day in which to sit down and think quietly of our beginnings and our ends; and each year that passes makes it more difficult to withdraw from the gathering roar, the accentuated speed, of human living.

The Preacher tells us: "Because sentence against an evil work is not executed speedily, therefore the heart of the sons of men is fully set in them to do evil." And there is more in it than that, for some of the sons of men will not wait for the leisurely processes of everlasting judgment; they want to take a hand in its execution. They see the evil done, and they are not content to rest in the Lord and wait patiently for him. They draw the sword and rush in. The moral status of men, as I have said, is on widely different planes; and is it to be wondered at that those who have achieved some painful inch of progress should leap to defend it against the inflow of a pagan wave ? I for one cannot wonder ; and this tragic contention of man with man would seem to be his fate for a long time yet to come, seeing that the levelling up of aspiration, which is the determinant of action, is not likely to be achieved within a measurable distance of time.

Accepting men as they are, and not judging them by the standard of what we would like them to be, we must expect to see the future world unroll its course in a fashion not dissimilar from that of the past ; and this will be constructed of three main elements : the men of love, the salt and savour of the race, of whom a handful will be born in any generation ; the men of formalised religion, who, because the light that is in them is darkness, will mis-represent the very core and marrow of Jesus's hard and strenuous gospel ; and the general race of men that Jesus loved, following the devices and desires of their own hearts, which are not always ignoble, measuring right and wrong by the rough-and-ready standards of temporal under-standing, generously willing, if need be, to die for what they conceive to be the truth, hating both the sin and the sinner, and convinced that the one can be extirpated or at least halted by the slaughter of the other. To God, I sometimes think, this muddled, fearless, battling and in-domitable mass of men must be at once the despair and glory of creation. Certainly its only hope, for of what use is leaven if there be no lump for it to work in ?

59

As for the true pacifist, the only representative of Christendom now living in the world, the man alongside whom, I suggest, the Christian church should be, but is not, ranged, his future is hard, rugged and thankless. The fighting, struggling mass of men are so many that they can point to some apparent *consequence* of their actions; the men of Jesus may well for generations have no more to show than a cross against a windy sky. Each of them, throwing his stone into the fetid swamp of contemporary life, may seem to do no more than raise a stink; but when enough stones are thrown in there is a way through the swamp; and when more still are thrown the swamp is gone. When we are offered so many precision implements, it is hard to fall back on the simplicity of steering by a star; but the star nevertheless is the only precision instrument that will resist change and decay until the heavens themselves shall be folded as a garment.

*   *   *

I shall no longer in this place consider those to whom ultimate truths are committed and whom we may not expect to be many. The men who affect the course of the world as in our time are men like ourselves, dirt with a rare vein of gold, compounded of good and evil, combatting the one and struggling towards the other according to lights that are dim, shifting and variable. Lady Monkswell, a Victorian whose diary has recently been published under the title *A Victorian Diarist*, tells how with her uncle she was visiting art galleries in Italy, and says : " Uncle Arthur's thoughts were divided in a very unequal proportion between Fra Angelico and an offer he had just had to sell Bryanstone Square."

We are, for the most part, caught in Uncle Arthur's dilemma. Our Angel Brother would like the whole of our attention, but always there is news from the mart to disturb the completeness of our dedication. "Late and soon, getting and spending we lay waste our powers." This is us, as we are, and as we must, somehow, get through most of our affairs. We shall, I fear, meet with little but disappointment if we expect men to be all spirit, as surely as the plotters of evil must now be disappointed, having reckoned on man's complete acceptance of smash and grab.

Sir John Hammerton tells in *Books and Myself* of a visit he made to Putney to dine with Swinburne and Watts Dunton. Watts Dunton pointed to the joint and asked, " How would you like it, Algernon ? " Swinburne answered, " Oh, give me a good bit of that fat—just like that I had last Saturday."

Recalling this domestic scene, Sir John writes : " This in his small piping voice, his eyes eager and expectant as he pointed with drooping forefinger to the coveted portion, seemed to me the absolute antithesis of any picture which the mind, unprompted by the reality, would ever compose of the passionate poet of Poems and Ballads and Songs Before Sunrise. . . . The foremost living poet, penultimate of the great Victorians . . . and a little bit of fat ! "

Well, I done know whether the mind, " unprompted by the reality ", would picture Swinburne demanding with passion goblets of nectar and ambrosia served on vine-leaves, with Hebe displacing poor Watts Dunton ; but anyway, the divine breath would soon expire without some sustenance for the body that houses it. That's how we are : Uncle Arthur's absorption in art is mitigated by the thought of a housing-deal, and Swinburne's body, small as it was, had to be kept together by cuts off the joint. Body and spirit dwell together.

*   *   *

We have got a long way from our starting-point, which was a letter to a newspaper saying : " There is a real danger to mankind in this tendency to relieve the professional soldier or airman of the normal dictates of conscience or of the proper exercise of free will."

I said that, in my view, soldiers and airmen could *not* be allowed to follow the dictates of conscience or to exercise free will, and that the first reason for this was that mankind was in a low state of moral development. I have tried to show that this is so : that in two thousand years the Western world has failed to put into practice the fundamental truth on which it is theoretically based : the truth which would make it in fact, as well as name, Christendom. I have tried to show, further, that there is no prospect, as we look about us in the world to-day, that there will be an immediate advance from this morally undeveloped situation. It is not my wish or intention to castigate men for being in a situation which I share with them ; I am concerned only to point out that the situation is what it is, that it is contrary to any situation which Jesus would have sanctioned, and that, this being so, we may expect (with a most lively expectation) that war will continue to be an instrument of human argument.

This brings me to the second point : that, if we are to have war, a soldier must obey his orders, whether he be a Rommel, or a Montgomery, or a private of the Buffs. War, which we all seem agreed is permissible, cannot be waged without unreasoning obedience. Tennyson has been sneered at for his " Theirs not to reason why ; theirs not to make reply, theirs but to do and die ". But he was (as often) in the rights of it ; for, if you are to have war, you must have this too.

There comes, in this country at any rate, a man's moment for the exercise of free will. That is the moment when he is at liberty to take the path of pacifism. Once that moment is past, obedience must be absolute. Otherwise, the nation as we know it is in constant danger of anarchy, and, such as it is, the nation is something of an achievement, a development from warring septs and tribes, that may well be a step towards coalitions of even deeper and happier significance. It must, in our present state of development, be preserved.

We should no doubt find it agreeable if Rommel and

other German generals turned upon the Nazi state and tore it down; this would nevertheless be a lesson in anarchy, and already liberated Europe provides us with lessons enough in that. How perilously frail the hold of the civil power on its army may be we have recently seen in Franco's Spain, and we nearly saw, in 1914, in Ulster. There can, I think, be no question whatever that a soldier must do what he is told to do. If it can be shown that he has exceeded the commission of the civil power, that is another matter, and the civil power must deal with him. But it is nonsense to suppose that in a society which has accepted total servitude the individual either in peace or war can enjoy freedom of will and conscience.

*   *   *

This letter to the editor of the *Daily Telegraph*, though it might as well be asking for the moon, does serve the purpose of showing what is present in many minds : a sense of the deep loss which a people inflicts upon itself when it accepts the obliteration of the individual. To be a member of an army pursuing a common end has its comforts and consolations, but it is significant to notice with what prompt alacrity the man or woman on leave sheds the uniform and looks out the slacks and the old tweed jacket. " This is me. Now I am myself again." Willing though corporate service may be, the deepest instinct in us is individual, and must be so. We are born one by one, and one by one we

die. In the rare moments of thought and solitude that
we permit ourselves we know this to be true. Some accept
it as a jewel beyond price ; others fly from it to the pursuits
of the mob, overwhelmed by the splendour of such solitude. It is one of the great facts of nature to which industrial society and " totalitarian " war do violence ; great
as the counterbalancing fact that the privacy of the individual life rots and rusts if turned too much inward, but
blooms and fruits if dedicated to the service of others. And
this service is not necessarily a conscious fussy matter : it
is achieved by the finest characters simply in the easy
natural process of being truly themselves. They tell us
now that the hips of a rose are full of nourishment ; but a
rose does not make the providing of nourishment its business. The hip is the outcome of a continuous unconscious
miracle of form and smell and colour, an unfolding from
root to flower, from birth to death. I have known men like
that : they said and did nothing to help me, but only to
know them *in being* was a blessing. And indeed nothing
can flow from us into another life save what is in ourselves,
and how full we must be before we can *overflow* ! These
are the lives towards whose shaping creation, if it has any
meaning at all, is directed : these flowers that bloom and
exhale fragrance, these lights that shine, this salt that
savours ; not the nuts and bolts that hold together the
rigid girders of regimented living.

* * *

One of the horrors of war is that, included in the great mass of casualties, there must be a proportion of this saving salt : not only poets and painters but men whose simple lives enclose the kernel of charity. It was customary between the wars to speak of those then growing up as " the lost generation ". It was the sort of phrase newspapers loved, and so it had a wide currency. There was something in it, and it is perhaps not fanciful to suppose that what was lost out of that generation was this leaven which is never too plentiful. It is one of the matters to be taken into account, when assessing the probabilities of the immediate future, that again we shall have a generation that is " lost " in this sense. There will be plenty of men, as there is plenty of musk ; but there will be a danger that, while the shape and common form of things remain unchanged, the fragrance will disappear, as, mysteriously, it disappeared from that homely plant. I read in *Country Life* a correspondent's guess that the fragrance of the musk and other flowers has gone because we would not leave them alone. There was a time when bees looked after the fertilisation ; then we took to propagating the plants by layering and cutting and what not. And so the fragrance, whose purpose was to attract the bees, disappeared, unwanted. Without pressing the point, without having myself examined all its implications, I throw out here the parable of a State husbandman whose scientific care for all may produce a condition in which everything in the garden is lovely save that the fragrance of personal charity is gone. And, if I have not charity, it " profiteth me nothing ".

66

And so it is a genuine reason for concern that the indiscriminate hook of war, laying low swathe upon swathe of common grass, may—indeed must—now and then cut down the finest flowering of the field of life. "From these and other operations all our bombers returned safely." The phrase has a comfortable sound to our ears, and no doubt—for English is not the only language in which it is written—to Japanese and German ears as well. It is good to know that all the bombers are back, that the young hazardous lives are, for the moment, spared to themselves and the world. But the bombs do not return with the bombers to England or Germany, to America or Japan. They have done their work, and for aught we know have put out lights that might have shone for generations, have extinguished sparks of grace that might have set the kingdoms on a blaze.

How much of this sort of thing can humanity—I shall not say Christendom—afford? Are we so rich? Are love and wisdom, art and skill, so plentiful? It is not surprising that Sir Osbert Sitwell should have advanced, in a book called *Letter to My Son*, the suggestion that some means should be found to keep artists out of the holocaust. I have not read the book, but I gather from a leading article in *The Manchester Guardian* that that is its theme, and that the *Guardian* thinks the argument "surely wrong". Sir Osbert, in a letter to the editor re-asserts his view. "Would you," he asks, "welcome the death of Shakespeare, in a tank battle, let us say, at the age of 30, while some minor official in a Government office was retained at home as being of 'national importance'? To think out some scheme to protect the artist is undoubtedly difficult, but he is of infinitely more value than the statesman, who seldom is himself expected to fight."

The problem, indeed, is "undoubtedly difficult", and not the least of its difficulty is in the very nature of artists who, despite a common notion to the contrary, are not soft and pliable beings, apt to take advice, however well-intentioned, even when directed to their own life's preservation; but obstinately resolved on going the way their *daimon* directs, which often enough is into the closest sharing of even the most bitter experiences of human life. Leaping into battle, as Julian Grenfell did, they cry : " If this be the last song you sing, sing well ; you may not sing another : Brother, sing ! " They will not rest but say with Jesus : " The cup which the Father hath given me, shall I not drink it ? " Somehow, I cannot imagine that Shakespeare would have chosen to remain at home and be attached to a Ministry for the " writing up " of the glories of our blood and state. Not even if he were permitted to wear a uniform and get salutes in the streets.

And another thing : what we are concerned with is not only the artist in being but the potential artist. As Herod sought out and slew the innocents—innocent, most of them, of any possibility of contributing much to the painful climb of the race—hoping that thereby he might destroy the small elusive spark of a great spiritual force not yet declared : so war mows right and left, and may well be

68

more successful than Herod in putting out for ever the flame that none has known to exist. Perhaps some child that has not even drawn breath on earth, but is shattered with the womb that encloses it, was the vital leaven that might have touched our common bread to sacrament.

Apart from these odd chances of disaster as war, blind as Samson, pulls its indiscriminate disaster about humanity's ears, there are those who are in the young bud of artistic promise—a bud so rathe and shy, so blown on by the cold March wind of adolescent timidity, that they nurture it secretly and disclose it to none. What of these? What are the saviours of the artists to do for them? You may be sure that they will not come forward and claim for their precious bud the protection of your cloak. They will take it into the heat of battle and there, if it and they be not destroyed—who knows?—that fiery blast may force it to its blooming. Those who, while not dying, have offered their lives to death, may experience death in the spirit and a resurrection in which all that they have and are bloom in a glory that might else have been denied them.

These are the tragic and moving chances that unfold as one considers the artist in war; and, for its full extension, humanity needs more than artists. The salt of the earth seasons many dishes, and some of them are very humble. The bearers to whom Jesus entrusted his torch were simple people enough. Perhaps in St. John there was the quality of flame that we understand when we speak of the artistic approach to life, and it was strong in Jesus himself; but

69

there is no evidence of it in any other of the disciples. And so to-day, if men and women are to be set apart for the sake of the world's joy and unfolding, there are many unknown to fame, many who never appear outside the "cool sequestered vale" of their daily lives, but belong to "nature's unambitious undergrowth, and flowers that prosper in the shade". These are they whose service is simply in their lives' unfurling; their unnoticed days are spent in a weary land where the breath of fame is not felt and the rumour of achievement is never heard; but there, to many, they are as the shadow of a great rock and as springs of living water. I have known such people; and I know that the putting out of their light would be as dire a loss as the death of many a man whose place, a hundred obituary notices would promptly say, could never be filled.

And so it would seem that to snatch artists from the furnace would not be possible without their improbable assent, and that even if it could be done, much material, as important as theirs, would still be shovelled in. What is roughly spoken of as "the balance of nature" suggests to the mind that, if the songsters are to flourish, you must not indiscriminately destroy even gnats and grubs. If "Thou shalt not kill" has moral meaning, the meaning must be absolute. Man who is capable of stoking the flames of war, is obviously incapable of deciding what, in the inscrutable working out of human destiny, is most worthy of survival. If we ("whose souls are lighted with wisdom from on high", as we sing so vaingloriously, with so little sense of the comedy we must make in everlasting eyes)—if we so act, Nature herself has shown no finer discrimination. Who knows what of beauty and truth has been cut off in its prime or before its blooming by her vast visitations of flood and famine, earthquake, fire and eruption ? And, to take the matter farther, who shall say what mute, inglorious Miltons might have found voice and glory had not chill penury, with the consent of the comfortable " artistic " few, repressed their noble rage ? The reference of the whole matter is wider than war : look where you will, the ground beneath the tree of life is white with fallen and aborted buds.

A broad conclusion appears to be that in this, as in so many matters, men can have what they like and take the consequences. Now a consequence of darkness is not an increase of light.

*   *   *

If we are to keep artists out of the holocaust, this could only be by the consent of the State ; and an examination of the nature of the State is not encouraging. There are many delusive notions concerning the State.

(I break off here to record a coincidence. I intended to make use of Macaulay's lines

> Then none was for a party ;
> Then all were for the state,

and I took down from the shelves, in order to verify the words, Thomas Babington Macaulay's *Lays of Ancient*

Rome, a book which I do not think I have opened for more than twenty years. As it lay on my desk—this old book which, I see from the inscription, my father gave me when I was eleven years old—the post was brought in. Among the letters was one of the nature that we call a " fan " letter, and it was signed " K. Babington Macaulay ". Whether this writer is a relative of Lord Macaulay I do not know, but it struck me as strange that, in the very moment when I was calling up one Babington Macaulay from oblivion, another Babington Macaulay should send me a word of cheer. In the realm of some ghostly supervisor it seems to have been decided that one good turn deserves another.)

Well let us go back and note that the delusions about the State arise from an overlooking of the fact that there are two questions to be asked : What is the State ? Who is the State ?

The State, to begin with, is a mystical body, and it is true of it, as of all mystical things, that most men do not think about it save in moments of crisis or emotion, and then, as again of mystical things, it is deeply powerful. It is this notion of the State that causes the poet to cry, " What can I do for thee, England, my England ? " or " Who dies if England live ? " It was round this idea that the nation rallied, without a rag of logic or reason to help it, after Dunkirk. It is a notion compounded of a thousand imponderable essences : it is nothing : it is everything : and it can command a supreme devotion. You might call it the soul of the nation, which being lost everything is lost, which being alive nothing can die. It cannot be defined. It must be accepted or rejected. "The glories of our blood and state." Such vague magnificent words seek to snare it, but it flies out of the net.

Such is the State in its mystical aspect ; and clearly this can do nothing for artists or for anyone else on the plane of the practical and worldly. It is not something that gives : it is something that demands. It gives only on conditions of submission, and then it can give nothing but virtuous intangibles.

What most people think of, when they speak of the State, is something that can give material benefits : houses and pensions ; jobs and family allowances ; roads and scholarships and exemptions for artists. And it is here that Macaulay's lines break down and the agreeable thought of none being for a party and all for the State does not look hopeful. For these benefits cannot be conferred by a mystical notion ; they must be conferred, if at all, by whoever happens at a given moment to hold the power of government ; and as it is in the nature of men that benefits are not conferred, or even promised, without some hope of return, the State under this aspect is a different thing from the State under the other aspect. Not a variation of the same thing, but a different thing, as, alas ! a monarch so often proves to be a different thing from the mystical notion of kingship. This State is something whose direction is determined by the mentality and the worldly possessions,

73

or lack of possessions, of the moment's government and of those who support it with their votes. Few men have the nobility to be concerned with reform as a pure conception, necessary because right. Revolutions and lesser movements of reform are rather to be considered as endeavours to transfer wealth and power from one set of men to another. That is why humanity is not on a road but on a see-saw.

So long as this method of procedure continues—and there is little promise of its discontinuance—*power* in the State, which is the thing that confers tangible benefits, will be concerned rather with such measures as may ensure its own prolongation than with the preservation of artists who, by the nature of their being, will not be deeply interested in the partisan aspect of politics. Let us imagine, as an instance, that it has been incredibly decided to grant pensions to a dozen men of letters. How long is that State patronage likely to last if all twelve of them sit down in happy leisure to write, say in a Fascist state, works on the virtue of liberty, or, in a Democratic state, works in praise of dictatorship ? No : the State's association with artists, as with the Church, can only be on condition that the State's notions are not sabotaged and subverted. And the State, in this second conception, being what it is, this is only common sense. We therefore reach the conclusion that the State, in its first aspect, can confer no material benefit upon an artist, and that, in its second aspect, it can confer none but material benefits, and that these will be conferred only on terms that few artists would accept.

74

What the State does for artists now—even for those whose works are untouched by political thought—is to let them quietly starve to death. It is just two years ago that I received a letter signed by John Masefield, Max Beerbohm, Walter de la Mare, T. S. Eliot, Edward Marsh, Compton Mackenzie, A. E. W. Mason, Arthur Quiller-Couch, Michael Sadleir, Bernard Shaw and Desmond McCarthy. It began : " One of the most distinguished men of letters alive in England, Mr. ——, will be eighty on March 3rd. He is still glad to work when he can get work, but he and his wife have no regular income except a Civil List pension, which cannot be increased, and on which, as everyone knows, it is impossible to live today." The letter went on to appeal for a subscription to a fund " to keep him from want for the next few years ".

That is what " the State " does for artists when in this green and pleasant land they are plodding across their sunset acre ; and when they are in more vigorous shape, how then ? My own experience has been that anything done for a State department, or for such great organisations as we may expect to see proliferate in the years to come, is paid for on a more niggardly basis than a private firm would think of suggesting. Consider, for an example, the London County Council : not a State department, but a comparable body. Two years ago the Council invited me to visit the County Hall to give a lecture " which would last about an hour or a little longer ". This was to be one of a course of six, for the benefit of teachers, " on the teaching of English in senior schools which, as you are doubtless

75

aware, have an age range of eleven plus to fourteen plus ". The letter ended, well in the tradition of letters from such sources : " I am afraid that the Council's scale does not permit the payment of a large fee, but I am authorised to offer an honorarium of £10 to cover your expenses. This is intended not so much as a payment for time and trouble involved, but as a token of the Council's appreciation of help."

Why on earth, one may ask, should there *not* be a payment for time and trouble involved ? And why should this wealthy organisation end its letter with what is virtually a whine for a free lecture ? To say nothing of the time involved in preparing an hour's discourse, three days would be needed to make the journey from Cornwall, deliver the lecture, and get back again. So what I was asked to contribute was : the time needed to prepare the lecture, the lecture itself, three days of my life, taxi and railway fares, hotel bills for a day and two nights. What the Council proposed to contribute was a " token " payment of £10. It looked a little odd to me, and added a postcript to my thoughts on the State and artists. Is it any wonder that at the age of eighty we send the cap round ? I hope that the official who signed this letter is pleased, as he goes home, at the week-end, to hear his token wages jingling in his pocket.

We have considered the State as a mystical idea and the State as paymaster ; and a line should be spared for the State as pay-finder. No word is more idiotically used than the word " State " in this connection. For example, in my morning paper I read : " State to shoulder bigger Share of Education Cost." Now in this third aspect the State is simply your purse and mine and our neighbour's. You may depend upon it that we shall not shoulder " the bigger share " of education costs, but in one way or another, we shall fork out every penny. And this is true of all other costs whatsoever. If we begin paying out more than we've got, we shall go bankrupt as surely as if the State were a corner greengrocer's shop. This is something to be borne in mind now that the air is dizzy with talk of costly reform. It is not an argument against reform ; it is an argument against illusion.

*   *   *

I have said that, in my view, the normal men and women of the contemporary world cannot, as things are, follow the heroic path that Jesus indicated. They must go on as they are doing, but seeking (or at their peril neglecting to seek) every foothold and handhold that will permit them, by howsoever little, to raise themselves out of the quagmire that we are content to call Christendom. But there is this that must be added : the night draws on. It is customary for the publicists and apologists of our way of life to speak as though we were at the brink of dawn. "Far off, through creeks and inlets making, comes silent, flooding in, the main." And so on. For myself, I do not see the

77

streaks of morning, but rather the confused congestion of a stormy sunset. We may hopefully assure ourselves, in the Psalmist's lovely words, that "the river of God is full of water", and indeed the individual soul may know that it is; but this great main can come flooding in to human affairs only through individual pipe-lines, and for the most part these are choked with the silt of self, the garbage of greed, and with muddy fears. All depends on their clearance, and the hour grows late.

*　　　*　　　*

This section is an interpolation. I had written another hundred pages or so of my manuscript when I read Mr. Michael de la Bedoyere's book, *No Dreamers Weak*. I turn back to tuck in here what I have to say about it, for Mr. de la Bedoyere takes this same view : that, when war breaks out, the Christian cannot go on living his life according to the will of Jesus. This would indeed seem self-evident, and it is strange to have to insist upon it : strange but nevertheless necessary, for it is by no means generally admitted that when a nation turns its whole resources to the task of becoming a death-factory it is acting offensively to the will of the Lord of Life. The appalling dilemma is that we have no option, and, though this—when we consider not the immediate origins and attributes of the present conflict but the long course of history—is something for which we as well as others must bear some blame, that does not help the matter. But at least let us recognise where we are and cease to live in the illusion that we blind, maim, eviscerate and kill to God's greater glory while our enemies do the same in the service of the devil.

However, let us get back to Mr. de la Bedoyere's book, for I wish to indicate certain disagreements as well as consents. This writer is a Roman Catholic, the editor of *The Catholic Herald*, and I have always found that what he has to say about the point where religion impinges upon daily life is worth reading. (But I am here speaking loosely, for he and I would agree, I think, that there is, or should be, no such specific point, but that religion is an essence that fills the whole house, like the odour of the broken cruse of spikenard.)

To begin with, Mr. de la Bedoyere agrees " with the pacifist in being unable to see how this domination of life (however well disguised the domination may be) by this fundamentally primitive struggle for survival—note how modern wars are actually called wars for survival by both sides—can be reconciled in any way with the spirit and teaching of Christ our Lord ; and how those who proclaim themselves His followers can also allow themselves to live their daily lives at such a degraded level ". (And, never let us forget that, despite the splendour of individual heroism and abnegation shining here and there, and the solid worth of a general steadfastness and resolution, the level of life in wartime is degraded, not exalted, because all these qualities should rightly be given to life, not to death.)

79

Having conceded that the pacifist, not the warrior, is the true interpreter of the mind of Jesus, the author goes on to insist that, things being as they are, there is no option but to set this true interpretation aside. Once war has broken out, " the one method which patently will not work in face of the real situation is recourse to the Christian way of acting ". Mr. de la Bedoyere extricates himself from this dilemma by taking refuge in what seems to him to be " a self-evident moral intuition, namely, that there can be circumstances when a people has no option but to take up arms ".

Here I am in agreement with him so far as the mass of us goes ; but it is at this point that, in my view, the Church —all the Churches—if they are to save their souls and in the long run save the world, must declare without equivocation that they are on the side of the pacifists. Otherwise, I am convinced, they will surely perish, and, even now, it is a question whether they are not too late, whether that organisation called the Church is not, by its refusal to take the hard way, reduced to a bubble, a simulacrum, which, apparently rounded and substantial, is destined to perish at a breath. If Christendom is indeed more than a name, the organisation which is its core, and round which our civilisation has matured, must surely reject outspokenly a way of life, which, in Mr. de la Bedoyere's words, cannot be " reconciled in any way with the spirit and teaching of Christ our Lord ".

The Church, of course, does not approve of war ; many

a priest and parson is riven to the heart by the agony of the contemporary dilemma which seems to thrust our breast, whether we would or no, upon the thorns of wickedness ; but all this does not meet the needs of our desperate case. The point is that there is no world-wide and august rallying-place for the many who are deeply troubled by the way in which the currents of life are hurrying at a pace which accelerates with the passing of these mechanically inventive years towards the thunder of the black cataracts of death. We have had organisations like the Peace Pledge Union, but that is not enough, as its collapse at the point of trial showed. It was weakened by its *ad hoc* and partial inspiration. We need something through which there breathes more than a negation, a fear of evil—something that is alive with affirmation of the beauty and truth of life in all its aspects, so that this rejection of war would not be a plank in a platform but a heart in a body : a body tactile to the good life at all points.

To give itself to this supreme endeavour, which would make the name Christendom something more than a dry wind sifting the historic dust of long-whitened bones, the Church would need a deeper inspiration than is now expressed in the mere deploring of man's tendency to sink below the level of his own finest moments. It would obviously, to begin with, mean dissociation from any State with which it might be connected, for the State could not allow a church affiliated to it to act counter to its own intention in a moment of physical peril. It would mean, too, a deeper degree of unity than the Churches have so far managed to achieve, but in the pursuit of so splendid an end there is nothing save truth itself that should not be gladly abandoned. And need anything be abandoned? Unity, when all is said and done, has nothing to do with uniformity. Let the jugs be of any shape you like so long as they are dipped into the well of truth. Amphora or egg-cup, it matters not. Each to the essence, and let God himself look after our queer, amusing, varying shapes.

Mr. de la Bedoyere is not with me here. "It is useless and false", he writes, " to try to prevent war by a pacifist condemnation of war as such and a pacifist resolution never to partake personally in war. One way of putting this truth graphically is to point out that a really pacifist country set in the contemporary, non-Christian world would have no survival value—scarcely more than an unarmed man living in a jungle."

There are several things to be said about this, and the first is that Mr. de la Bedoyere does well to say that it is of no use to condemn war *as such*. You might as well condemn diphtheria and do nothing about the drains. I have tried to point out that, in my view, a pacifist attitude involves a definite stand on the vast and complex causes that swell the tumour and lead to the inevitable ill. Neither the Church nor anyone else can be allowed to draw in its skirts from the consequences of its own apathy and acquiescence. It is to be understood that the pacifist attitude of the Church would be not a discrete and *ad hoc* sour disapproval of violence, but, as I had put it, the operation of a living body, tactile to the good life at all points. This would be the sufficient sanction for its final stand.

Secondly, Mr. de la Bedoyere speaks of the difficulties that would beset "a really pacifist country". But in my vision, the question would not be that of one pacifist country facing an aggressive neighbour; rather of a solid body of pacifist feeling in *all* countries. It is in order that this may be secured and fostered that the task belongs to the Church, which alone is in the position of having all lands to work in and the whole of spiritual life for its province, so that pacifism would fit into its place and not be, what it has tended to be, a mere sore thumb on a body not, anyhow, attractively healthy. There is, in these days, something remarkable and abnormal about a pacifist. His pacifism, more often than not, is unrelated to a general spiritual health and normality. It "sticks out a mile", as they say; and in a harmonious personality nothing does that.

The third and most important point arises out of Mr. de la Bedoyere's reflection that a pacifist country, in a non-Christian world, "would have practically no survival value".

What is survival value? Does nothing survive when our blood and bones are dissolved? I imagine that the Roman soldiers, dicing at the foot of the Cross on Good Friday, had little belief in the survival value of Jesus. But what survived—and from small beginnings—was the

83

whole conception of life resting within the scope of the word Christendom that haunts these pages like a ghost doomed to disappear at cock-crow. And the cock will be the one that announced Peter's betrayal of his Lord. But the Church lasted a long time; and it can continue to last on a condition; and that condition, I suggest, is that no matter what the odds against it, the "survival value" of a complete acceptance of the teaching of Jesus should continuously be put to the proof as the story of mankind unrolls. Here, I know, I shall differ widely from Mr. de la Bedoyere's orthodox Catholic view; but I do not think it is enough (save for the refreshment of soul to be found in a mystery) that we should take refuge in "the one oblation of Himself once offered". The man who would follow him, said Jesus, must "take up *his* own cross". The Cross is still upon the hill, and our "lesser calvaries" avail. These, too, have "survival value".

*   *   *

I know that there is a common and widespread reply to those who are prepared to use all measures in opposition to war, and this reply is based on what I take to be the false assumption that if we disapprove of the use of "totalitarian" force we must therefore disapprove of the use of any force whatsoever. And so this reply usually is a question such as this : "What would you do if you saw a bully twisting a little chap's arm?" Well, I would do my best to restrain him, even punching him in the nose if that would help.

This is not a matter in which we must be so inelastic as to tie ourselves up in the shackles of an unbending logic, insisting that a consideration applying to a large case must necessarily apply to a small one. After all, we are entitled to use our common sense in deciding any matter on the basis of what, obviously, its consequences will be. Because I am unprepared to shift a stone whose removal will start an avalanche is no reason why I sould not shift ten or twenty stones that are common stumbling-blocks to me or my brother. And, equally obviously, to punch a common bully in the nose is an action having no possible moral or physical parallel with setting on the march the enormous forces of national and international destructiveness. Surely these are matters in which we must use our humour and common sense.

No, indeed ; there is no case for saying that in no circumstances must force be used in the world, and those who take the extreme attitude of saying that I am wrong here, that *any* use of force is undesirable, must face the fact that there is such a thing as non-physical force, which they themselves constantly use. This, as Jesus recognised, may be more important than physical force which can affect only our bodies. " And be not afraid," he said, " of them that kill the body, but are not able to kill the soul : but rather fear him which is able to destroy both body and soul in hell."

85

It is hardly to be contended that, because this non-physical force can be harmful, it should therefore not be exercised at all. We are all of us, consciously or unconsciously, exercising it in every moment of our lives. A parent is exercising it when he decides what school his child shall go to, under what religious system, if any, his child shall be brought up, what cultural influences shall surround him in the home, and if the child, now a youth, is so pliant as to have few notions of this own, the father's "moral suasion" may extend to so vital a matter as the career the boy will pursue throughout life, and the marriage he may make.

Here, if you like, is force in being; and its extension into the national life, by means of education and "propaganda", is there for all to see. This force, like physical force, can be good or bad. In the one instance and the other we have the responsibility of deciding each case as it arises in the light of its possible consequences. Now it seems to me that to punch a bully in the nose, or to take the chance of a few cracked skulls by ordering a police-charge against disturbers of the local peace, is not a matter within the same range of thought as unleashing essentially blind forces which will hammer and batter throughout the world, by earth, air and sea, destroying millions of lives, millions of homes, the treasures of time and art, until, both the blind forces being too exhausted, bruised and bloody to go further, one retires murmuring "Victory" and the other "Defeat"—words that would seem to have little meaning to any pair of ears not " conditioned " to the slogans of one side or the other.

*　　　*　　　*

I am not suggesting here a cure for the world's ills. If you want those, you can have six for a penny in the pamphlets and proposals of planners and politicians. I am suggesting something which, to begin with, will probably never be tried, and which, to go on with, has but a hardy and desperate chance of success even if it were tried. The difficulties would be great and many. Let us suppose that the first obstacle had been overcome and the necessary unity of action had been agreed upon by the Churches. This would mean that, in peace time, the Churches would dissociate themselves from all that had to do with armaments and associate themselves with all that had to do with the promotion of brotherly relations between the peoples. It would mean that the teaching of Jesus was expounded not only as a set of general moral principles but as an ethic touching national and individual life at every point. The squire's lax understanding of the responsibilities of property-holding, and the " City's " dangerous meddling with the lives of vast populations in the interests of investors, would be matters of the Churches' concern, and so would any parliamentary action which tended away from righteousness. Only by preoccupation with all these things, which are the seeds of war germinating in time of peace like maggots burrowing, hidden by profitable wool, down towards the very vitals of a healthy-looking sheep, could the Churches justify the final stand that they would have resolved to make.

All this, it may be objected, is nothing but to ask the Church to take up that " mere " humanitarianism which, it says, has already failed. But if humanitarianism has failed, it has failed not because it was ignoble but because it was partial. Its aim, the good of man, is a worthy aim of any endeavour, and it is not for the Christian to dismiss it as common and unclean but to adopt it and enshrine it within the body of his wider conception, remembering that the saying " Man does not live by bread *alone* " implicitly tells us that he does live by bread. There is no reason why a Church, giving up nothing of its sacramental activity, should not realise that the ultimately sacred thing is human life itself. Man and not God is the material of our endeavour. God is. We can do nothing to diminish or enlarge Him. But the spirit of truth, working through us, the Word made flesh, can enormously enlarge man's accessibility to God, and it is hard to see how the Christian can dismiss as not within his province any deed of mercy, love or justice, any opposition to a personal or national way of life which denies these.

That is one thing, and another is that these subtle and furtive germinations in the fair-seeming body of peace are the causes of that final disruption, that utter negation of the teaching of Jesus, that we call war. If, then, the Churches

88

should resolve to stand firm in opposition to the effect, they must logically concern themselves with the causes.

I have said that their chances of success are small ; and, indeed, I think that if success were to come at all, it would be only after a long and fluctuating struggle. It is probable that the Churches acting as I have suggested would at once lose large numbers of members, and, almost certainly, these would be the richest members. And then, when the time of testing came, there would be in all lands another heavy falling off. Once war had broken out, all the allurements and allegiances that draw men to the national cause, away from the cause in which is neither Jew nor Greek, would be felt with the accustomed force. But if the Churches as Churches stood firm, if the banner remained, no matter how few saw the matter to an end, then, once the war was over and the inevitable frustrations and disillusions again sent their chill winds rattling through the hollowed minds of the people, once the sad eyes of humanity again pondered the stone it had received instead of bread, there would be a flocking back, and this time in large numbers.

So it would go, with the Church of the Prince of Peace swelling in peace-time, losing numbers in war-time ; but gaining ground with each test survived, until, *in a very long run*, it would be a force too great for the temporal masters of the world to ignore. Long, tedious and exacting as this process would be, I see no other which offers a chance of ultimate peace on earth. I see no organisation, among those which we know in the world to-day, sufficiently widespread, hallowed and august to undertake it except the Christian churches. I see no faintest hope for the survival of the Christian churches unless they undertake it. Nothing can survive in mere suspense. It must fight against its opposite. Death is the opposite of life, and it was life more abundant that Jesus came to bestow. Death more abundant is the promise of the embattled power-states. There can be no discharge in this war.

For myself, I see little hope that the Churches will address themselves to the task. Their tide is at too low and sickly an ebb to float such argosies. But this reflection need not bring us to despair. I am not of those who believe that on a given date, some two thousand years ago, in the cowshed of a Jewish village, God first entered the life of mankind. I believe He enters the life of mankind with every breath man draws in love and truth and beauty. His purposes were at work before the Christian church was conceived and will be at work when it is a memory and legend, if that should prove its chosen fate. By what new methods those purposes would then be achieved we cannot know ; that they will be achieved it would be presumptuous to doubt ; that man, His reed, so fragile yet capable of such sweet airs, will remain His instrument, is a dear hope. But this would not be necessary.

> Who fathoms the eternal thought,
> Who talks of scheme or plan ?
> The Lord is God ; he needeth not
> The poor device of man.

90

In the vast perspective of cosmic space and eternal time
—(if I may be permitted to marry so ill-assorted an adjective and noun)—it is not difficult to conceive of man
and his planet, or even all that part of the cosmos which
he apprehends under the name of his universe, as amounting to little more than a sand-castle whose span of glory
is but the distance between two tides. The " poor device ",
so proud of its own subsidiary devices, its restless going out
after many inventions, may prove too poor altogether : too
poor in spirit because too rich in pride, too possessive to
relinquish and renounce, to realise that having nothing it
has all things, and that the way to survival is not by domi-
nance but by absorption into the universal purpose of life to
God's greater glory.

*   *   *

All this has left out of account another element of the
matter, and that is the attitude which the modern power-
state is likely to adopt towards the Churches, should they
decide to set themselves counter to its intentions. It is
not likely that the Churches would be allowed to proceed
far upon their road. We have entered a phase of history
when the tension between one man and another, between
one state and another, and between the state and its insti-
tutions, is what we choose to call " ideological ". The pattern was set by France of the revolution, and the central
notion is a conviction of final rightness. No longer is the

nation seen as a mixed wood, with forest trees rising here and there, with undergrowth of one sort and another, with the spring flowers blooming out of the mat of humus. Now the nation is a wood as conceived by a mathematical forester. He has decided what tree is best for that soil and he proceeds to plant it. There they are : the long straight lines of spruce or fir, or whatever it has been thought best to grow. There is no give and take, no elasticity : there is a plan, and what does not conform to the plan must go. This way of looking at life did not last long in France. France had the spiritual vigour to deny that final rightness can be achieved. Her people asserted their liberty to chop and change, to try this and that, to re-establish the mixed abundant ecology of national life. Perhaps they did not overtly understand, but they happily apprehended, that interdependence of all types gives better promise of human happiness than the deliberate breeding of one type. They believed, in short, in the sanctity of the individual man and woman.

But while the wild men were in command there was a violent set against the Church, and this happened again in Russia when the revolution broke out there. Because the Church, by its very essence, must be opposed to a mathematical conception of human destiny.

It is not the thing at the moment to utter so much as a murmur that could be interpreted as a disparagement of any part of the Russian exhibition in contemporary life. There is indeed a nauseating tendency, especially among

our "intellectuals", to hover around Russia with the in-
gratiating alacrity of junior clerks anxious to have the privilege of holding a match to the new boss's cigar. In the
long run, this will do no good either to them or to Russia.
Russia is still a most secret country of which we know little,
and she seems resolved to keep herself so. Stalin's Mona
Lisa smile may reveal to us, as Leonardo's lady did to Pater
(if to no one else), that he "has been a diver in deep seas
. . . and trafficked for strange webs with Eastern mer-
chants", but beyond such romantic and recondite speculations it is not easy to go.

What bears upon our point is the indubitable fact that,
though the Church in Russia was permitted to exist, it
was, at first, subjected to such indignities as "anti-God"
exhibitions, and then was, by "the Party", esteemed of
so little worth that, to this day, so far as I know (and, as
I have said, one is not permitted to know *certainly* much
about Russia) no man is allowed to belong both to it and
to "the Party".

There is abundant evidence that the Church in Russia
before the revolution was, for the most part, an ally of
oppressors, a nest of superstition, an organisation that a
clean spiritual vision would look upon as besmirched and
befouled. But I do not think it was because of any of
these things that the Party decided to have none of it. A
totalitarian State—which is to say, a State in which all
must move in one direction—cannot afford to have any
truck with an organisation whose fundamentals include,

93

or should include, a recognition that " the wind bloweth where it listeth ".

There is, now, a more cordial phase of recognition between Church and State in Russia. They are exchanging bows. I have pointed out elsewhere the significance of the moment at which this has been achieved. The Church is with the State in the prosecution of the war. But what I am considering here is the condition of things in which the Church refused by so much as a hair's breadth to help the State in a warlike purpose, and made clear in peace-time what its war-time attitude would be. I do not think the Church in Russia would survive on these terms, and, with the growing totalitarian direction of the great nations, our own included, it would be hard put to it to survive anywhere. The general contemporary tendency is towards " total " states, immense power-units, centrally driven towards purposes in which the people have little to say. They may think they have much : they may think they have " made up their minds " about this and that : but, in fact, their minds have been made up for them by incessant doses of press, wireless and cinema propaganda directed from the centre. It becomes increasingly difficult for an effective " opposition " to be staged to any State activity in the modern world. For the Churches to stage one against the Moloch of our supreme and suicidal devotion would be to court almost certain extinction. But what a death ! " For whether we live, we live unto the Lord ; or whether we die, we die unto the Lord : whether we live therefore or die, we are the Lord's." What could not spring from the ashes of such a phoenix !

*   *   *

There is that in the atmosphere of our times which drives us back upon first principles, makes us seek to clarify the things that matter to us, and above all, to define our terms, in so far as they can be defined. Not that our deepest compulsions spring always from things that we can see and handle and explain. But this, too, must be stated and accepted. In the preceeding pages I have used such words as "God" and suggested that there is such a thing as the "spiritual life". "God", in particular, is a word which can be used with distressing looseness to mean anything or nothing, to sanction any situation. I suspect that this is why Christendom appeals to God more often than to its founder, Jesus ; for Jesus uttered words that we can take hold of and examine and assess. But when these words condemn us, we slip nimbly past them and appeal to "God" who may be anything : for example, a Jahweh, mighty in battle, not greatly distinguishable from Odin, Thor or Wotan. Nevertheless, we must continue to remind ourselves that "Christendom" is not a society founded on an acceptance of the fact of God, but a society pledged to the acceptance of a particular view and interpretation of God : the view of Jesus that God is the loving all-father and that therefore all men are brothers.

95

I shall try presently to say what I mean by some of the words I have used. That is often necessary, despite the people who have invented the "science" called semantics, which seeks to make every word say just what it means, and neither more nor less. Poor fellows! They have a hard task ahead, for they are asking language to do both more or less than it is capable of doing. When I read Keat's *Ode on Melancholy* I find these lines :

> Ay, in the very temple of Delight
> Veil'd Melancholy has her sov'ran shrine,
> Though seen of none save him whose strenuous tongue
> Can burst Joy's grape upon his palate fine ;
> His soul shall taste the sadness of her might,
> And be among her cloudy trophies hung.

What, I wonder, would a "semantist" make of those last two marvellous lines ? Here, I fear, words must be allowed to say more than analysis can detect ; and, indeed, "He that hath ears to hear, let him hear" tells the "semantists" what folly they sponsor. They remind me of a book I read whose author was "Mass Observation" (!) and which explained the Roman Catholic Mass by describing each physical detail of its administration. The little fellow behind a pillar with his note-book must have been a comic figure.

And so, lacking precise semantic skill in scoring a bull's eye of meaning with every word I write, I shall presently have to elaborate some of my terms, and even then perhaps not leave them clear. But before I come to that, it

96

may be profitable to put down as true a record as I can of
the religious influences that bore upon my own life. For,
in many particulars I suspect, my experience was not unusual. It may serve (always with personal reservations)
some purpose of general illustration.

This story begins in the last decade of the nineteenth
century. I was five years old in 1894, and that was the
time for going to school. I attended a board school in my
native town—a town then of some 200,000 inhabitants—
and this board school, which I left when I was twelve
years old, was the only school I ever attended. Was I
given any rudiments of religious teaching in this school?
I do not remember. Memory, with me, is a capricious
faculty. Last night I came upon a reference to the town
of St. Omer, and I remembered that during the last war
I had spent some months there. Turning those months
over in my mind, I found that there were happenings as
clear as daylight, and others blotted out as though they
had never been. I could not, and cannot, for one thing,
remember where I messed or billeted. Whether in a house
or a barrack, a farm or over a shop, alone or in company :
it is completely gone. So with my infant school. I can
remember a day when I was in the "babies" class, and it
was bitterly cold, and a glorious fire was burning in the
grate, and the teacher, whose name was Miss Bates, looked
easy and motherly, and I was filled with a sense of happiness. I can remember another day when the midsummer heat was so oppressive that every child had the fidgets,

and the teacher said : "The quieter you sit the cooler you'll be." I can hear now those very words, though I cannot remember who spoke them. I can remember a recurring horror. Each child was given a box of square bricks to build with, and when the time came to put the bricks back into their box, it must be done thus. The bricks were arranged in a cubic heap on the desk and the box was fitted over the top of them. The lid of the box was held in the left hand at the edge of the desk, making an extension of it. Then the bricks under the box were drawn by the right hand forward till they rested on the lid. Holding the lid under the bricks and the box on top of them, one then righted the whole thing upon the desk and pushed the lid home in its groove. It seems a simple if unnecessary manœuvre, but I could never bring it off. There was always the tell-tale clatter upon the wooden floor as the bricks failed to meet the lid, always the burning sense of shame at failure.

Such things—many of them—memory recalls with precise detail ; but it does not recall whether we ever sang a hymn, or had the Bible read to us, or were in any way taught the religious rudiments. And the point, I think, about this hiatus in memory is that there is no hiatus where something significant has been put in. From this I conclude that either there was no religious instruction, or that, if any were imparted, it was done in a way that failed utterly in its purpose.

That, literally, is all that can be said about religion so far as my schooldays went.

In our home there was no religious teaching or influence. My father was a sceptic, if a rejection of the divinity of Jesus (in the theological sense) be scepticism. I know this because I recall hearing my father say to my mother that " Jesus was a man like any other ". My father was not a man who discussed such matters—or any matters— with his children. He was an aloof reserved person, feared rather than loved ; and so, beyond a recollection of this phrase, I have no knowledge of his mind in matters of religion. It would be possible to deduce too much from it. I know that he never attended a church service, but, having an interest in the occult, was sometimes at spiritualistic *séances*. So to that extent his mind was not wholly material, and this deduction is strengthened by a knowledge that he read much in Milton. I still have his hard-used copy of *Paradise Lost*. He died when I was a child, and I can say that his life had no religious influence on mine, unless within that term we may put this : that he, before anyone else, directed my mind to good reading.

My mother, who survived into a great old age, dying in the year in which I write this, had spent some years of her childhood in an orphanage, and she would tell me how the 'orphans, in their drab uniform clothes, were " crocodiled " on a Sunday to the church near the orphanage and seated there *en bloc orphelin* under the supervision of a person whom my infant mind conceived as a beadle of the Bumble type (for we early took to reading Dickens). I imagine I was not far wrong in this. What religion my mother absorbed from these Sunday mornings I do not

99

know. She brought up her large family with a Puritan morality. Foulness of speech was unthinkable in her presence ; theft or lying somehow could not exist near her ; and her own indomitable stoicism, that made her fend for the family with a spartan vigour, overflowed to us. Thus I recall that one day, playing in the board-school yard with my elder brother before the school opened, I threw him to the ground heavily. Clearly I had hurt him. He winced with pain, but, saying nothing to anyone, sat through the morning's schooling. When he got home, he was marched to the doctor, who found that his arm was broken.

Of religion, as I am writing of it here, nothing was imparted to us by our mother. Like my father, she attended no place of worship during my earliest years, nor do I see how she could have done, for throughout the whole time till my father's death there was a nursing baby in the house. And as my parents did not go to church, so the church did not come to them. I recall no single visit to the house by clergyman or minister. The " highways and hedges ", from which the wedding guests were to be summoned, did not include our street.

I fall again into my habit of divagation to ask whether it was to be expected that the parson should visit in such a street as ours ? It was a street of people who were poor, and for the most part uncouth, and for some part violent and blasphemous. Though I lived in this street throughout many of what are called the " formative " years of my life, and though to this day I understand, I think, a good deal about the sort of people who live in such streets, I should feel awkward and unsure of myself if I tried, now, to establish a friendly relation with them. How much more must this be so with a parson whose background had always been different, whose culture was of a different order, and whose social education and aptitude, so far from fitting him to deal with such a situation, un-fitted him for doing anything of the sort ?

In one of those books, significantly frequent nowadays, in which parsons deplore the shortcomings of their own church, I recently found it said that the worth-whileness of a parson could be judged by the number of times he had a labourer to dinner. Now this seems to me to be nonsense, unless the parson is a saint, and few parsons, or laymen, are that. A saint may be expected to have the common touch that permits him to be easy with all men, recognising their oneness in the eye of God, and the power not only to be easy himself, which is not the difficult part of the matter, but to induce an answering easiness in the heart and mind of his companion. If this grace be absent—and to possess it is the rarest of gifts—an endeavour to bridge social and cultural differences can result in little but a false heartiness that rings as hollow as a tin pot. Your labourer would be the first to detect it ; and on his side, too, there would be no outflow of personality, no grace or easiness. In the generality of cases, contact is far more likely to be established on a casual than a formal occasion : a chat under a hedge, a meeting in a field. My own most intimate talk with the parson of my village took place when we both sought refuge from a storm in a wayside hut.

An interesting book by Hugh Massingham, a son of the famous Liberal journalist, was published some years ago under the title *I Took Off My Tie*. The author told how, distressed by the gulf between the poor and the well-to-do, he sought to bridge it by going to live in the East End of London. The experiment was not a success. He could take off his tie, but he could not take off his accent or anything else that belonged to what we call a man's culture, and he met with little but suspicion and mockery.

Disraeli talked about the two nations that live side by side in England. There are not two, but at least twenty-two, and the gift of sliding in easy intercourse from one to another is denied to most of us. Shaw says in *Everybody's Political What's What?* that once everyone has an income sufficient to guarantee all the necessaries and comforts of life, it won't matter a straw who has a superfluity, for the securing of the necessaries will remove the bar to marriage from one class into another. Once society is thus brought into flux, our present rigidities will disappear.

This is true if we bear in mind that the root of the question is not money but culture. The average dock-labourer of to-day has a higher income than the average parson, but this does not diminish the sense of the gulf between them. The gulf will be diminished, and at last abolished, when those necessaries and comforts which

Shaw wants to see equalised are understood to include the manners, physical, mental and spiritual, that "makyth man".

This diversion leads me to conclude that if no parson sought us out in those early days, the fact leaves nothing for wonder, the world being what it is. We should have been as uncomfortable with him as he, no doubt, would have been with us. If a parson had asked my parents to dinner, they would, I feel sure, have been abashed, flabbergasted, and would have found a way to refuse.

*   *   *

My first contacts with religion as a force consciously seeking to disseminate certain principles of living, were thus not made at home or at school. It is for sectaries to decide whether those first contacts, when they came, were fortunate or unfortunate. They came through the Salvation Army and the Plymouth Brethren.

Every Saturday night the Salvation Army, with its big drum and braying band, took up its stance outside the public house in our street. I am trying to discern the impact of religious influences on my early mind, and the Salvation Army made none. Its coming was welcomed, but only as a show, a diversion. A band and uniforms of any sort will always attract children, and these attracted me. The girls with their fetching bonnets and clashing cymbals, the men with their hearty shouts of "Halle-

luiah ! " and " Praise the Lord ! ", the occasional ecstatic
breathing of the name " Jesus ! " with upturned eyes :
these were exciting ; and so was the moment of tension
when the pennies began to fall on the resounding taut
skin of the drum laid in the middle of the circle. Would
they amount to the two shillings, the half-a-crown, or
whatever might be the " target " that the leader urged the
on-lookers to attain ? And was it quite playing the game,
when the half-crown had been reached, to raise the sum
to three shillings ? It was as thrilling as an auction sale.
The drinkers would come out of the pub and throw their
pennies, which, with the price of their pints, may well have
been wanted at home, though such a consideration did not,
then, enter my mind. All that was present was a noisy
excitement that culminated in the moment when the drum-
mer picked up the drum, the party formed into ranks, and
with a *boom, boom* and crying of brass they marched away,
singing a hymn, to their barracks. I was often of the
straggling tail that accompanied them as far as the doors,
but I never entered their hall, and remember those occasions only as a noisy show.

*　　　　*　　　　*

I began to know the Plymouth Brethren through their
Sunday School, and I went to Sunday School, with my
brothers and sisters, because poor people with large families like an hour to themselves on Sundays. I do not think

104

there was more in it than that. Certainly, there was no discrimination. Nobody in our house said : " Well, the time has come for these children to have some religious instruction. What is the best place to send them to ? " The point was that the rectangular drab chapel of the Plymouth Brethren was the nearest place to the house—but a stone's throw away—and so the children would have the least chance of being run over or coming to some other harm.

The other day I was repairing a pergola that the wind had blown over. It is impossible in these days to buy wood, and so, when the job was done, it was a poor botched-looking affair. I said so to the jobbing gardener who was helping me, and he answered : "Ah, well, sir, the uglier the better, they say." I had not heard this blasphemous proverb before ; perhaps it explains why Cornish people put up, with no sense of disquiet, with the ugliest houses in Britain, painted, usually, in the drabbest colours, a muddy brown or a grey that is almost black. They do all they can to disfigure the glory of their own landscape. Anyway, if I were to try, looking back across the years, to assess the attitude to life which the Plymouth Brethren inculcated, I should sum it up in that life-denying saying : " The uglier the better."

I should not like to do an injustice to a whole sect. It may be that there are Plymouth Brethren and Plymouth Brethren. I never learned anything about the central government of these people, if there is one, and possibly there are reckoned within their boundaries congregations into which some sweetness and light have penetrated. What I have to say refers only to the congregation I knew.

Their chapel, to begin with—and I soon knew it as an attendant at the morning and evening services as well as the afternoon Sunday school—was a grim depressing oblong box. It was simply that : four flat walls, with a few tall windows on one side, drably coloured, completely unadorned, furnished with brown-painted benches. The atmosphere was penitentiary, and no doubt was intended to be so, for this was a penitentiary religion. Joy was frowned upon, and as joy will, sometimes, creep into the hearts of young things, an abominable hypocrisy was there forced upon many children as their means of escape. To the normal benighted mind it may, for instance, seem that a child may play football and yet escape the pit, but it did not seem so to these people. The more docile of their young accepted this ban, but there were spirited children who kept football shorts and jerseys at friends' houses, changed there before and after a match, and let it be assumed at home that they had spent their afternoon in a country walk.

If football was a sin, the theatre and dancing were hell itself, and it was inevitable that, listening to this kind of doctrine week after week, one came to accept much of it. Save in the case of football, there was no countervailing influence. Our board school had a soccer team whose red and white shirts were to me as important as any national flag. The doings of the team were a matter of debate among boys and teachers alike, and this overbore the chapel doctrine, so that, Brethren or no Brethren, I was a keen supporter, though never a player. But so far as the theatre and dancing went, there was no one to suggest to me that these things were not necessarily inventions of the Devil. I believed that they were, and thus my life was truncated. To this day I have never learned to dance, and it is late to begin; and my adult love of the theatre is perhaps a re-action from those days of repression.

To digress again, what am I to do about this liking for the theatre now that I live in a county which, I think I am right in saying, has not one theatre within the whole of its boundaries ? It has buildings—yes. In my neigh-bouring town of Falmouth there are two buildings which once knew the living drama and now are cinemas. But "the theatre" is not only a building. I pick up a book and find it entitled *Théâtre Complet de Molière*, and this "théâtre" of Molière is nothing but the work which Molière wrote. If ever the question of a national theatre comes to the stage of solution, I hope it will be solved with both the component words borne well in mind. "Na-tional" does not mean "metropolitan" and "theatre" means more than a building. Those who live in London —and, for that matter, in Manchester, Birmingham and many other large towns—have the theatre conveniently with them all the year round. But there are millions of our nationals—and, being one of them, I make this case self-

107

ishly—who are starved on this side of their existence. A truly " national theatre " would take as its first duty the meeting of this need. " Ensa " has shown that it can be done in war-time ; the Russians had already shown that it could be done in peace-time, for they had the habit of sending the best of their music, ballet and theatre circulating to their remotest territories. There is no reason why a county like ours should not have a dozen or a score of theatrical companies, and orchestras too, visiting the places which, otherwise, must peg along with an unenlightened backwoods mentality. And the same thing applies to the national art collections. The " Rutherston Collection " of works of fine art, circulating through a wide area from its centre in Manchester, is an example of how the thing could be done. It is time to irrigate the desert. We provincial Arabs cannot be expected all to make the journey to the Nile and our local oases are thin and insufficient. Much is already done for the body : it is time something was done for the mind and spirit.

*   *   *

I was never, formally, a member of the Plymouth Brethren sect. There were two stages by which that formal membership was attained, and I did not pass through either. To begin with, one became " saved ", and this salvation was never a matter of patient education in the hard life of the spirit : there must always be a moment, like Saul's on the road to Damascus, whereon the believer could place his finger and say : " It was there and then—at that instant of time—that I passed from death into life." It was customary to record this moment in a Bible, thus : " John Jones, Born August 10, 1880. Born again, November 3, 1899." Having been born again, the believer made his public testimony by baptism, which was by complete immersion in a tank under the floor at the front of the chapel.

I did not, I say, pass through either of these experiences. My place in chapel was always behind a notice, half-way down, which read : " Unbelievers, sit behind this seat." But enough of the mentality of these people seeped into me to make it easily possible for me, even now, to understand a state of mind which would ask, with genuine surprise : " How can looking at a few pictures do anything for the spirit ? "

I am trying to answer all the questions that arise in this book by reference to personal experience, and so it must be now. Though I have never been able to put two lines together in a drawing, or match two colours in a painting, pictures allured me from childhood. There must, in my board school, have been some attempt to teach the elements of drawing, because I remember trying to copy, with " shading ", a cardboard cone that was set upon a desk in front of the class. But that is literally all I can remember of this subject. No one ever showed me a good picture and tried to make me see for myself why it was good. I would, as I grew up, stand for long times outside print shops considering the pictures in the windows, and I visited again and again such public collections as there were in my native city. But these were poor, though there has been an improvement since.

When I left home in my early twenties and went to live in Bradford, my lodgings were near Manningham Park, and the Cartwright Hall in the park had a fair collection of pictures. Moreover, there was an " annual exhibition " which I looked forward to with excitement and attended with enthusiasm. I got to know that gallery " by heart ", and I have only to close my eyes now to see the olive green bookcase in Will Rothenstein's " Browning Readers " and the blue gleam of the spread silk skirt in Wilson Steer's " End of the Chapter ".

But this was all fumbling. And then one day the newspaper I was working for sent me to Leeds to interview Michael Sadler (I do not remember whether he was then knighted), the Vice-Chancellor of Leeds University. What the occasion of the interview was has passed from mind. All that I recall is Michael Sadler and his pictures.

Reading this week Q's posthumous volume *Memories and Opinions*, I came upon a passage in which the author speaks of his first evening in hall on his arrival at Oxford. " We freshmen ", he says, " dined on that night at an island table set along the middle of hall and were joined by three or four seniors who had come up for the tail of the Vacation to read in the quiet of Oxford at that season. Fortune gave me a seat beside one of these—now known to fame as Sir Michael Sadler, his own distinctions, enhanced through parentage of a distinguished son—but for me then yet more of a demi-god—a third-year man, pride and hope of Rugby and (to cap all) President of the Union. Yet, as it were casually and without condescension, or more than that of an elder brother, he drew into our talk another senior man on his right and presently the two together were advising me on small practical matters . . ."

I do not know how many years passed between Q's meeting with the young Michael Sadler and my meeting with the by then famous Vice-Chancellor. They must have been many, but the man had not changed. *As it were casually and without condescension.* The words were still true. He was a great collector of pictures. The room in which I met him contained many : some hanging on the walls, some propped against bookcases. Whatever business it was that took me to see him was soon despatched, and then, "casually and without condescension", out of his own overflowing love for them, he talked to me about the pictures. Is it too much to say that this was one of the fructifying moments of my life ? I do not think so. For the first time I looked at pictures through the eye of a great amateur and connoisseur. The words of that friendly discourse are all gone : the spirit of the moment can never be taken from me. I never saw Michael Sadler again. I cannot think of many men with whom one brief contact could be so fruitful. When I ask that question : "How can looking at a few pictures do anything for the spirit ? " it is of that moment I think ; and I nourished the hope that pictures circulating through the country, with some such lover to speak the right words about them, may awaken a mind here and there to go out upon its own discoveries.

*   *   *

How few men I found, as I went about my work as a newspaper reporter, who had the gift to depart, " casually and without condescension ", from the immediate issue and to talk as man to man ! William Temple was one of them. I recall how, busy as his life must have been when he was Bishop of Manchester, he did not dismiss me after the matter that had called us together was ended, but charmingly talked of books and this and that. On the other side, consider an experience that befell a colleague of mine. A prominent Manchester citizen had rung up the office and asked that a reporter be sent to see him, as he had some matter to impart. My colleague went, knocked at the great man's office door, and entered. He had advanced half-way across the carpet when there came a barked Prussian command : " Halt ! " He thought for a moment that this was a joke ; but no, the fellow was serious. My colleague not only halted, but about-turned, rightly, quick-marched, and refused ever thereafter to see the person who had these strange notions of how to receive a fellow human being. This person was noted in the city as a Liberal humanitarian, full of notions for the advancement of mankind. I once heard it said of him : " He doesn't suffer fools gladly," which is usually another way of saying that a man has a damned bad temper, a good opinion of himself, and no manners.

* * *

To go back to my Plymouth Brethren : I have said that I believed the theatre to be the devil's domain. I was still attending that chapel when I left school at the age of twelve and went to work in an accountant's office. I recall how I was walking to the office one day with another office boy, and we passed a hoarding on which was a bill advertising our local music hall. The time was to come when to attend music halls would be both my duty and my delight. I would attend three in one day : a matinee in the afternoon, a first and second house at night ; and write about them for the *Manchester Guardian.* There can hardly have been a " turn " on the halls that I did not know better than most people. Lauder and Robey, Little Tich and Harry Weldon, Grock and the first George Formby, Harry Tate and Wilkie Bard, Vesta Tilley, Clarice Mayne and That, Hilda Glyder : those and many others were in their hey-day, and I loved them all. Looking back, I sometimes wish I had expressed my love with more candour, but I and a few others who wrote for the *Guardian* about the

113

halls were young and full of our own importance and believed that severity was the mark of good criticism. It was
our policy to leave no turn unstoned—or few turns, anyway. We ran to a certain extravagance. One of us, I remember, wrote of the " egg-shaped personality " of Little
Tich : an escape into surrealism which must have caused
that great comedian's strange blue baleful eye to burn
when he read it in the morning. I should try to-day to
write on that subject with more wit, if possible, and with
less solemnity, which would be easy.

But all this was far in the future as I stood that day
looking with my friend at the bill on the hoarding. The
turns to be seen at the Empire were listed there, and, heading them, was that of the Ten Loonies. My young companion said to me in a man-of-the-world voice that he had
been to the Empire last night, and added that the pranks
which the Ten Loonies were seen to be playing in the pictures on the bill were nothing to what they did in fact.
Upon this casual declaration, it would not have surprised
me to see the paving-stones at that boy's feet split asunder
and the flames of hell lick about him. This in the most
literal and factual way. It was strange, uncanny, to see
him standing there, to all appearance a normal boy. He
was laughing at the recollection of what he had seen the
Ten Loonies do, incredibly unaware that these clowns
were imps of Satan, devilish sprites luring him to the edge
of destruction.

Indeed, it was always strange at that time to notice that

114

the people who indulged in those sins which the Brethren denounced were, apparently, normal. If they talked to you, no fire came out of their mouths, you could smell no singeing on their clothes, and they seemed kindly and reasonable. At the same time, there were members of the congregation, men who sat among the elect in front of the notice, confident that they were "saved" for time and eternity, who were not kindly and reasonable. There was one, I know, whose children lived in fear of his belt and whose wife was not immune from an occasional clout. There were others who seemed to me sly, or bombastic, or silly. Of them all, there was but one, a board-school teacher, who had my personal liking.

They were mostly people of the artisan and small tradesman class. Only one, in my recollection, was of any standing. He was a manager in a firm at the docks, and, if one may judge from the house he lived in, a well-to-do person. He often addressed the congregation—anyone was free to do so, "as the spirit moved"—and always in a pompous high-flown fashion. Memory furnishes a phrase from one of these addresses : "As an illustration, let us assume that I should give my daughter a pearl necklace—though God forbid that I should do such a thing."

I remember how this man was once making a commentary on the life of Jesus, shown to us in a series of "magic lantern" slides. In one picture Jesus was standing in Jordan, with John the Baptist pouring upon his head the water of baptism. We all knew that this was wrong.

Baptism as practised in the Church of England was sinful. The *compère*, I think, had not bargained for this slide, but after a moment's embarrassment he came out magnificently : "This picture tells you how the Devil represents our Lord to have been baptised."

This was the man who—God forbid!—would not give his daughter a pearl necklace. The wearing of jewellery, any sort of personal pride or adornment, was another sin. It was hard to move in that environment without barking oneself on a sin. The Wesleyans, whose chapel was not far off, were crusted with sins like an old hulk with barnacles. Everything they did was wrong. They sang "Amen" at the end of their hymns, and that seemed to the Brethren dangerously liturgical. They wore top hats on Sundays, and that was a sin of pride. Their parsons read their sermons, and that was a denial of the command to speak as the spirit moved. In those sermons, poetry and references from profane writings might be found, and that was a failure to see that The Book contained all that was necessary for salvation. Worst of all, their parsons were paid. They were "hirelings". It was not a thought that would occur to a child, but it has occurred to me since to wonder what the Brethren would have said had it been pointed out to them that Jesus was paid for his ministry. Money is no good until it is translated into such necessaries as food and lodgings, and if these are freely given, without money as an intermediary, it amounts to the same thing. Certainly, once he had entered upon his ministry, Jesus

116

did not practise his trade and was kept by his followers.

The strangest matters came under debate in the chapel. One of the Brethren—a leader in that Israel—kept a religious bookshop, and a hot debate once blew up about his wares. For, as well as Bibles and tracts, text-cards to hang on the wall and such things as that, he sold profane literature. It is necessary to understand that this particular congregation, at the time I knew them—and all I write here is limited to that—were maniacs about the Bible. There was no light—not a spark—to be found elsewhere. No exposition or exegesis, however humble, reverent or inspired, was admitted to be anything but a devil's device to lead away from the Book. They would themselves get up, "moved by the spirit", and tell you exactly what the Bible meant, and it did not enter their thick obsessed heads that thus they were doing, in their sufficiently unimaginative fashion, what some of the loveliest minds had tried to do in the books they condemned. I hesitate to give one example of their own exposition : it is so incredible, so banal and idiotic, that I should not believe it if I had not heard it. It was the custom to hold Bible readings in the vestry on week-day evenings, and I attended some of these. A chapter would be read line by line, and after each phrase there would be a pause for comment. The line had been read : "There shall be no more sea." There was a pause for the hallowed minds of the Brethren to examine this. At last one of them said : "Therefore we may take it that there will be no more fish."

This was said with no facetious intention, with no wish to make a poor untimely joke. It was said seriously; seriously it was accepted; and the reading proceeded.

Such exposition then was to be accepted, but exposition in a book was damnable. And the Brother whose books were in question when that quarrel blew up, was not even selling such books as these : he sold fiction ! And to read fiction was comparable in enormity to taking a hand at cards or attending a dance. Often I had paused before that Brother's shop window and examined his stock-in-trade. The fiction that caused the uproar was simple indeed : it was the stuff in large type, bound in highly decorated boards, gilt-edged, that was at that time in demand as Sunday School prizes : Hesba Stretton, Silas K. Hocking, Annie Swan and Mrs. O. F. (*Christie's Old Organ*) Walton were typical authors. It was the sort of thing that would have streamed the tears down the rugged face of a Bret Harte miner. But if it had been written on the screen of doom with a stick charred in hell it would not have been more sinful to the Brethren.

I do not remember the upshot of this particular hulla-baloo ; but the matter was of importance to me, for though my infant mind was warped, dutifully accepting as God's gospel truth much of the blasphemous nonsense taught me, there was one point at which I was blessedly free from infection. At that time, and for long afterwards, fiction was a master-passion of my mind. My father, who had done nothing about my religious instruction, had at any rate given me a taste for the best novels. I was reading Dickens and Defoe, Bunyan and Swift. In some obscure shrine of my being, I worshipped the men who wrote these books and felt that if any men on earth were worthy of emulation it was these. By the grace of God, the Brethren, trampling on any fingers that clung to a fragment of sweetness and sanity, never made me let go my hold there.

After the Sunday evening service in the chapel, the Brethren would trudge in a ragged procession to a spot near the gateway into a small park, and here an open-air service would be held. Dutifully I would trudge with them and stand in the ring as they bellowed their version of salvation's path. I hear, even now, one of those voices booming into the sweet summer evening air "If you don't believe you'll be damned! If you don't believe you'll be damned!" in raucous senseless iteration ; and one of my intimate nostalgic memories encloses a moment in which that voice, or another, ceased, and from within the park gates came the sound of water tinkling into a pool, dripping from the upraised fingers of a little naked boy in bronze, and then of even that sweet sound ceasing as the gardener turned off the fountain, and there was nothing but the warmth and quiet and mystery of the summer night. I think that in my childish way I must have come to have a sense, never perhaps defined, that what these people had was not a militant but a wrangling religion ; and I know as a fact that those open-air meetings near the little park had much to do with my salvation. For this, beyond doubt, was a religion to be saved from—this religion which consisted in little but finding beams in others' eyes while stridently crowing about the perfection of one's own spiritual vision. It lacked all that a man needs : beauty, humility and love.

When all that striving and crying at the street-corner was over, I would slip alone into the park where the evening shades would be deepening, so that the water of the pond would be black, for many trees grew about it, and the swans would seem the whiter, moving in their stately way to their resting-place on the farther bank. The park, altogether, became the symbol of another way of life. It was the place where lovely things happened and " peace came dropping slow ". There was a sundial with the old hackneyed motto " I only count the hours that shine ", but it wasn't hackneyed then. I had not come upon the words before and they suggested something gracious. I know now how futile they are, and what gold may be mined from the dark rocks of sorrow and adversity, how foolish and frivolous the life may be that only counts the sunny hours. But a little gaiety, foolishness and frivolity was then, had I but known it, my need. The sundial helped, and the park helped altogether. The smell of the grass as a small leather-booted horse pulled the mower over the lawns, the fountain with Goscombe John's gracious little boy, sleek and shining as a seal in the water, the great clumps of " red-hot pokers " burning in a blue autumn dusk, the sight of the man who had given the park to the public exercising his right to ride his horse therein—a white horse, and on it this man, who was always hatless, with close-cropped snow-white hair and a hale austere face that I now know to have been like Emerson's : all these things made the park precious. It became a sanctuary, which is a place where one is safe because within the embrace of holiness, and in the last few dusky moments before closing time on summer evenings there was to be found there this comforting sense of everlasting arms.

*   *   *

So I grew into my 'teens, and then, unsaved and unbaptised, I left the Brethren. How or why I cannot recall. Perhaps it was incompatibility of temperament. I imagine I just walked out as, out of a house in which the wrong woman has trapped him, a man may walk and never go back.

Since I am here examining the effect upon my life of the religious influences beneath which it has been spent, or at any rate of the influences that called themselves religious, I must try to determine what legacy six or seven years with the Plymouth Brethren bequeathed to me. First, I think, a distrust of religious *profession*. A man's creed is what he says he believes ; it may even be what he thinks he believes ; but I have learned to look elsewhere for what in fact he does believe—if anything.

(This is true also of those national creeds that are baptised with the hideous name of ideologies. To make decisions about a country, it is necessary to go behind that façade and discover how, at home, the people live, and whether, abroad, neighbours, especially poor and defenseless neighbours, are treated with consideration or arrogance. If it appear to be a government policy to put barriers against my freely arriving at decisions in such matters, then there must be a suspension of opinion, tinged with scepticism.)

Those who, in a truly religious sense, have any belief whatever are, I have come to think, appallingly few : appallingly in face of the enormous darkness they are called upon to lighten, the stupendous inert lump in which they must work like leaven. And that, I believe, is the only way in which spiritual truth can be imparted. The man who is in God feels no more need to shout and strive than the sun does when it rises over a summer hill. First he swims against the stream, then he swims with the stream, then he *is* the stream. And in that stream others may plunge. That is the way of it, and a slow way it is. But I don't think there's any hurrying it. On this day when I write I see reported in a newspaper a statement of Lord Cranborne's in the House of Lords. He is speaking of the evils rampant in the world, and says : " If the peace settlement is to succeed, and is to pave the way to better times, we have got by some means or other to stamp out that corruption of the human spirit."

See the vagueness of it ! " By some means or other." The speaker has no idea how the task is to be fulfilled, but by some means or other " we " have got to " stamp out that corruption of the human spirit ".

This I hold to be a futile and fallacious approach. It is the righteous Plymouth Brother crying on the street corner, out of the fullness of his belief in his own virtue, that " if you don't believe you'll be damned ". It must be assumed that " we " (again, I suppose, the " we whose souls are lighted with wisdom from on high ") have the cure, but we are not certain what it is—only that " by some means or other " we must " stamp out " other people's corruption.

" Stamping out ", I fear, will not do the trick. There is only one way to overcome corruption, and that is the way in which one clears up a dark spot in a garden. The light of the sun is caused to shine upon it. That is all. Or, as St. Paul expressed it simply : " Be not overcome of evil, but overcome evil with good." This is an unpopular remedy, because it shifts the onus from somebody else's " corruption " and gives us the job of being so uncorrupt that corruption cannot exist in our presence. How long is it going to take to cleanse the world by this mere contagion of righteousness ? A longer time than most of us have the patience to contemplate. But when you think how long man has existed on this planet, and think further how short a distance he has advanced upon his road, you will see that a great deal of patience may yet be necessary.

123

Morally, man still plods like a tortoise, though mechanically he can fly like an eagle. But a tortoise flying in an aeroplane is a tortoise none the less.

It is remarkable how we delude ourselves that our mechanical advance is an advance of civilisation. Nearly all that we rely on for our salvation at the moment is a series of elaborate devices for throwing things at one another. It is humiliating to consider dispassionately how much human ingenuity has been expended on nothing but that. First men threw stones at one another with their naked hands. Then they devised slings, such as David used to slay Goliath. Thus they could throw things from a greater distance. The ballista improved the technique. Now the distance was greater still and the missiles heavier. For closer work they could still throw spears and javelins, but (as the idea always was to throw something that would kill from a distance) the javelin was narrowed down to a slim sharpened wand that was called an arrow and could be shot out of a bow. The discovery of gunpowder enabled the missiles to be thrown from the greatest distance yet. There was the small missile out of the flintlock which developed into the rifle-bullet, and the bigger missile out of the first clumsy cannon that developed into the high-explosive shell. Then came the grenade and the small bomb that could be thrown by the hand : and ingenuity next devised a means of throwing flame.

It took many centuries to reach this modern pitch, and in the meantime we had built navies whose business was the same one of throwing things : the ships first threw solid cannon balls and then explosive shells at one another and at the enemy's ports. Now these missiles can be thrown at targets so distant as to be invisible, detected by apparatus of an inconceivable delicacy and complication, and the ingenuity that devised these things is still at the service of a moral condition which, in this matter, has not arrived a whit beyond that of the cavemen who threw rocks. We are doing what they did : throwing chunks of stuff at one another.

Then we learned to raise ourselves from the earth and the sea, and we took our moral manners into the air with us. We could now throw things down. But as we all learned to play the same game, the fighter came up to frustrate the missile-throwing of the bomber, and so we began to throw things at one another in the air as we had done on the land and sea. The instinct to throw without being thrown at, which caused all the advances in stone-and-iron-throwing technique, then caused the Germans to devise their "robot" planes. These could be thrown at us with no men in them. The Germans advanced beyond this with their " V " weapons. The " robots " travelled slowly enough for detection and intervention to be possible, and so the method of throwing had to be improved. Now the missiles come faster than sound and we have the consolation of being killed without knowing what hit us. These " V " missiles, the scientists tell us, are to be the thing of the future, swifter and more accurately addressed.

They will come out of nowhere to a precise target, and in that sense, they will be, morally, on the plane of a stone thrown over a wall by a hooligan who knows he is going to smash an unseen greenhouse.

Is it not a little humiliating to reflect that from the first stone thrown by an angry semi-ape at his brother to the latest battleship or bomber, men are settling their quarrels by a method which, morally, is now what it was then ? I at any rate find it so.

The scientists themselves are a little perturbed at the consequences of their restless prying, and it is right that they should be. Their defense is that their business is discovery, and that what use humanity makes of the thing discovered is humanity's affair : a defense I find as convincing as a Borgia's defense would be who said he had done nothing but put poison in the cup, and if his guest were fool enough to drink it that was his own look-out. And in any case, the defense does not take into account that, whatever pure science may do, applied science has for long and consciously given its attention to means of destruction, to their making and marketing. Fulton offering his submarine to anyone who would buy it, Napoleon or Pitt, is a case in point.

Not that science concerns itself wholly with destruction. Its constructive benefits are clear, and should be gratefully acknowledged. For example, it has learned, I read, to turn beans into wool. It now only remains to turn wool into beans for our joy to be complete. Because then we shall have both beans and wool, whereas now we have only wool and beans.

*   *   *

The other thing I learned from the Brethren was that " the uglier the better " was not a doctrine I could live by. I had not then heard that " Beauty is truth, truth beauty ", or considered its implications (which all lie beneath the surface, wrapped up in the call to worship God in the beauty of holiness) ; but at any rate I felt in my bones that ugliness was not truth—else, as I see it now, this would be a most truthful world. Then, I was concerned only with what one may call the surface pattern of Keats's saying, and that, too, has its part in the wider and deeper whole. The wretched buildings in which the Brethren met had not even the beauty of austerity. It had nothing but a flat unimaginative power to depress. To sit in it for an hour was like spending an hour in the company of a bore, and to do that, even to-day, when I have resources against boredom, makes me feel as though fungus is growing on my soul.

Something more than a dismal building was involved. I was beginning to discover some beautiful things for myself, apart from the intimations that visited me in the park. I have told elsewhere [1] how, at about this time, a lodger came to live in our house, bringing with him a crate of

[1] See *Heaven Lies About Us.*

books, and how he went soon after, leaving the books behind him. They were immortal stuff that lit up my imagination. I believe that from the earliest years those who are at all sensitive to such matters have what may be called a feeling for authenticity. They don't need to be told by a professor or anyone else " This is the right stuff ". They *know*, which is the inner meaning of the saying that a man can learn nothing that he doesn't know already. All the genial wooing of the sun and all the kisses of the rain can get no more out of an acorn than the oak tree that is miraculously folded up within its shell ; nor will they get less, if they are given their way.

Not that, at that time, I was imbibing nothing but blushful hippocrene. Far from it. I was in the full welter of chaos. In any given week, I could read one of those penny magazines for boys that had such names as *The Gem* and *The Magnet*, and a novel by Henty, and Meredith's *Ordeal of Richard Feverel*. And, what is more, enjoy all equally. Equally but differently. That is the point. One difference was that there could be no difficulty in comprehending what Mr. Henty was saying ; but with Meredith there was difficulty enough. Difficulty enough, but passages where the impact of beauty was absolute, and you *know* that beauty was something valid, final and unquestionable. I do not know how far this tangle of incongruous attractions is characteristic of adolescence in its earliest stage. It is as though one followed and dabbled in many little streams, some cloudy with mud, some clear and sparkling enough, but all shallow and chitter-chattery, till a stray surge from the ocean came in here and there to impart a new taste, exciting but incomplete, and till this, in turn, gave place to the overwhelming experience of the deep and salty sea.

This, more or less, is how it was ; and it was in a half-way confused condition, when the novels that the Brethren disparaged, and the poems which they despised, seemed to me to say something more real and pregnant than I learned in their grey-painted coffin of a building, that I left the Brethren and went elsewhere.

*   *   *

I shall diverge for a moment to look at the complete casualness of my experience thus far : its lack of premeditation, motive or plan. I have written elsewhere of the force which, consciously or unconsciously, parents exercise upon the lives of their children. This matter of religious training is an important case in point. In my association with the Brethren, and, as we shall presently see, with the Wesleyan Methodists, I was acting under what may be called the force of indolence. This was content to leave me to the force of chance, which can be of primary importance.

Round about our house in those days, within easy reach of a pair of young legs, was almost every church you can imagine : Roman Catholic, Anglican, Baptist, Presby-

terian, Salvation Army and Plymouth Brethren. Chance,
which took me to the Brethren, might as easily have taken
me to the Catholics, who were pretty strong in our town.
Our great local landowner, the Marquis of Bute, was a
Catholic, and the annual Corpus Christi procession, wind-
ing its picturesque way through the streets, to end up in
the peacock-haunted grounds of his lordship's castle, had
a quality that could easily have attracted my allegiance.
As it was, my romantic mind drifted weakly under the lash
of an extreme Puritanism : not the Puritanism of Milton's
scholastic bent but rather of Fundamentalist darkness ;
and this has given to my mind a warp which can never be
wholly eradicated but is perpetually in conflict with the
weft of an innate disposition towards what Matthew
Arnold called, for want of a more precise definition, sweetness and light. Thus, I feel, the fabric of my being can
never be completely integrated. I shall always be a Greek
with a strong dash of the literally God-fearing Jew.

And if chance could produce so strange and desperate a
hybrid, could it not have done with me also any one of a
remarkable number of things ? I pondered upon them as
I listened to the Brethren expounding the doctrine of
Election. There was no doubt in the mind of any one of
them that he was of the Elect. Backsliding there might
be, a recession from the fullness of that high calling, but
there could be no final slipping out of the hand of God.
The Hand was under you, like a hand under a tickled
trout, and in due time it would land you on the green
pastures of Paradise.

130

It was a comfortable belief—for the Elect. And, as the Duke of Wellington said of the Garter, there was no damned nonsense of merit about it. You were, by God's grace, of the Elect, or you weren't, and that was all there was to be said.

It was here that the stupendous possibilities of chance plagued my young soul. For all I had had to do with the matter, I might have been born a Chinese who had never heard of redemption ; I might have been born in any one of the endless ages before Jesus appeared upon the earth. What then of Redemption and the Elect ? Were all those countless generations damned to hell for ever ? I did not see any alternative if this doctrine were true ; and since, even in our own day, one had no say as to whether one were born into the bed of a Plymouth Sister or the Catholic Marchioness of Bute, the stupendous force of chance seemed to weigh as heavily on the next world as on this. For it went without saying that a Catholic could not escape hell through the luck of being a marchioness, with a few castles to live in and gardens full of peacocks.

If chance had placed me in different hands which had taught me simply that God is love, and that, despite the annual tons of exposition, exegesis, and scholastic and theological guesswork in general, all we can ever know of God is what we may learn by living a life of love. . . .

But speculation upon the tricks and wiles of chance, upon life's incomprehensible and unpredictable Ifs, is of all occupations the most vain. Let it be enough to say that some instinctive revulsion of spirit made me reject this meat and look elsewhere for nourishment. One of my sisters, much older than I, was a candidate for baptism, and was, in fact, baptised later. But before that happened, there being in the minds of the Brethren grave doubts as to whether she was in truth " saved ", whether the signs of God's election could indeed be discovered in that young life, much debate sprang up. I remember delegations of these obviously commonplace and stupid fellows coming to the house to cross-examine and exhort, full of an indefensible pretence to an apostolic authority to decide between God's sheep and goats. It was at once nauseous and comic, the last straw upon a back already badly suffering from the hump, and I took myself along to the worldly, wicked, music-playing and Amen-chanting Wesleyans.

*   *   *

If you know the picture of Wesleyan Methodism which Arnold Bennett has painted in his *Clayhanger* trilogy, you have only a partial notion of the matter. Bennett *hated* Methodism. (The word is his own.) Clearly, chance drifted him that way, as it drifts all of us in childhood; the chance of what our parents and guardians think is good for us. When he was old enough to find his own path, he broke from this scene of his youth. There is no evidence in his books that he found for himself any substitute for what he then abandoned, except such vague emotionalism as is expressed in *The Feast of St. Friend*. In his journal he tells how he was wandering alone one Sunday night in London and halted outside a Nonconformist chapel whence the sound of hymn-singing reached him. Recalling the moment, he says : "And I hated the thought of my youth."

It has always seemed to me that these few words cut deeply into the core of what I have always thought to be the tragedy of Arnold Bennett. How far it was tragedy of character and personality I have no means of knowing, though I imagine it was that, too. Here I am thinking of the tragedy of the man as a writer. Many cosmopolitan and metropolitan minds are born in the provinces and find release and fruition when they have dried their wings and flashed out of that sphere. I think the reverse was true of Bennett : his personality did not assemble itself, come together, cohere, as he moved farther and farther from his origins. It flew apart and dissipated itself in bright profitable *trivia*. He was a "born provincial" if ever there was one. His understanding of provincial life was both passionate and profound. All his threads, all the ducts through which vital nourishment could reach him, led back to the Five Towns, but perversely he would not have this. He saw himself as a suave metropolitan connoisseur. If he became aware of a remaining provincial wart, he took the latest beauty treatment to remove it. He strained all the threads, and finally cut them one by one ; and then, as I see it, he was finished, stranded in his artificial world of yachts and babylonish hotels and fabulous incomes, totting up with an ant's industry the daily output of words, words, words. His rise towards fame (on the wings, be it noted, of his earthy and provincial inspiration) chanced to coincide with the demand by wealthy newspapers for "big names" that must be paid big money. He became snared in that web. He lived up to his conception of himself as a *grand seigneur* of letters, involving himself in large expenses that chained him to the duty of their discharge. Working even in such conditions, he was immensely readable, a conscientious writer, a reproach to many who decried and envied him. Personally (if a sole brief encounter permits me to express an opinion) he was a man who conveyed an impression of strength but at the same time of friendliness and goodwill. His tragedy was that the youth which he hated was his essential root, and he cut himself deliberately clear of its possibilities of power and refreshment. In my view, a few of his things will long survive, and deserve to : *The Old Wives' Tale*, the *Clayhanger* trilogy, a few short stories and *Riceyman Steps*. With the exception of this last, all these are the vital juices of his youth distilled into art ; and *Riceyman Steps*, it is significant to note, has nothing to do with the world of flambuoyant fancy that he had created for his ego to inhabit, but is down to rock-bottom among poor struggling men and women. When I consider the great mass of Arnold Bennett's work, I think how much poorer we should have been had Thomas Hardy persuaded himself that to depict the world of grand ladies and big houses was, somehow, more befitting a gentleman of letters than to write about peasants living in cottages under the Wessex Weald. Not that Bennett handled his material with the awkwardness of Hardy in his moments astray. He moved with ease and conviction through his far country; but the feeling remains that, for him, it was a far country, and that English literature is the poorer for his desertion of a talent that, in his day and of its kind, was entrusted to no one more richly. Yet my last word on Arnold Bennett must be of gratitude for what he did rather than of regret for what he chose to leave undone.

*   *   *

A Wesleyan minister who, from those days till his death, was my valued friend, once told me that his father, also a Wesleyan minister, had done a turn of service in the Five Towns. This old man could recall a day when he watched the children rushing in glad release out of a Wesleyan Sunday school. Outside the school, leaning against a wall, watching the scene with an intense absorption, was an ugly youth, one of the Sunday school teachers. This was Arnold Bennett, who was to learn to hate all that the moment stood for. "He seems", said my friend, "to have understood everything about Methodism except its soul."

It is possible that the setting had something to do with it. Bennett's early environment, and the environment of

Methodism within it, was physically deeply repulsive. In my case, this disadvantage did not happen. The Wesleyan chapel I came now to know was in a graceful part of our suburb, and our town altogether had none of the satanic horror of the Potteries. Such industry as there was, was light and scattered. The town lived mainly, like a comfortable *rentier*, on an income that derived from other people's hard work, dirt and danger. We were, in effect, little more than a mouth through which the black riches of the South Wales coal-mining valleys spewed themselves to the sea and thence to the ends of the earth. At the docks you could watch the coal-waggons tipping their contents on to the chutes that slanted down into the holds of the ships. A certain amount of dirt was necessary there; but it was localised; for the most part it was a clean town, with trees growing in its main streets, with a sight of the sun going down behind Garth mountain to cheer the eye, away beyond the gleaming reaches of the Taff, in the heart of the town. Of a summer's night, at the very crux and confluence of our main highways, you could hear the cold inhuman screech of his lordship's peacocks, and look up to see the time told upon a golden clock-face in his lordship's tower, shining through the unpolluted air.

From time to time, the source and origin of our well-being would stir, now sending its hosts of little, dark, mufflered, capped men down into our streets on the occasion of an international Rugby match, now on occasions less propitious. One such occasion I remember, from a time when I must have been very young, and even into our poverty-stricken *cul de sac* there came day after day bands of these little dark men, with their women and children, singing the intolerably moving songs and hymns of the Welsh ; and when I asked my mother the meaning of this, she answered briefly that there was a strike " in the hills ". And a bitter, belly-emptying strike that was, as I have learned since.

But, in the main, we lived happily apart from these troglodytes delving in their dark ducts and subterranean galleries. It was a town of happy southern climate. Much blue sky and warm air has a place in my memory of childhood, and almond trees that bloomed early in suburban gardens, fantastically beautiful in the light of street lamps. The Wesleyan chapel, as I recall it, was a building with some beauty of its own, an affair of honest comely stone, with broad stone steps (which can be so lovely) reaching up to its front door. And the whole thing was placed inside a small rail-enclosed patch of green grass in which many tall trees grew. In the basement rooms, which were used for odd casual purposes, these trees, as a summer evening was fading, would make a cool subaqueous green dusk, which, by a trick of memory, is one of the things I most closely remember of the chapel.

There would come a moment in each service when the parson would read the announcements, and every three months or half-year—I forget which—this would be among them : " Pew rents are now due. The stewards will be in attendance on such a date to receive same." The structure of this announcement is worth considering. Its phraseology is commercial. "To receive same" is the good safe jargon of a business circular, and the members of this congregation were, almost to a man, good safe well-to-do commercial people. Devonshire and Cornish names were common among them, for though Cardiff is in South Wales it is not *of* South Wales. The great names in the commercial life of the town were not, in the main, Welsh. Cornwall and Devonshire, offering small chance to those of their sons who did not take to the sea or the land, explored across the narrow water of the Bristol Channel. The Welsh in the "hills" were the labourers; the invaders, for the most part, filled the commercial and professional offices.

But our congregation, as I shall now call it, had no professional element, so far as I can recall. I have no memory of a doctor or lawyer, a journalist or soldier. They were business people, and most of them would be called in the North "warm" men. (There is a lovely phrase I once heard in the North—on a Derbyshire farm. The farmer, a woman, was speaking of the good fortune of her grandchild, whose godparents, uncles, aunts, and what not, were all contributing, on birthdays and Christmas days, to the child's bank account. "They're all in good gets," said the farmer. That is the only time I heard the expression, and it serves my turn now, for it is enough to say that our congregation was made up of people in good gets.)

I am writing now of the first decade of this century, and

138

of the opening years of that decade. World War I was not
far away, with its disruptive charge at the very foundations
of a way of living. But no one would have imagined this.
Twenty years after the time of which I write, our city,
notable now for snug unadventurous security, would see
rocket millionaires soaring aloft, throwing off dazzling
sparks that many fools rushed to gather, to find their fingers
burned and to see the rockets explode and disappear like
the pretentious nothingness they were. Great wealth for
a few (and for a moment) and deep poverty for many, were
to follow upon this poised, comfortable, "warm" and
guinea-guarding moment of which I write. It was to me,
who had then left the city and watched the spectacle from
afar, of a deeper interest because I had played in the back
streets with one of these masters of financial jugglery whose
name became known throughout the country before it
fizzled out like a firework in a puddle. His father, a labouring man, was none other than one of our Plymouth
Brethren, and young Tom, as I shall call him, accompany-
ing his father to the services, was known to us children
(with what seems now like prophetic insight) as the Fiery
Serpent. This because of the fervour he imparted to his
singing of a hymn :

> Bitten by the fiery serpents,
> Many dying lay. . . .

He was always what we should then have called "a bit
of a toff", and I well remember a local crone chiding me

with the words : " Ach, you dirty boy ! Why don't you try to look a gentleman like little Tommy——"

We did not guess that the time would come when the Fiery Serpent would be living upon an august estate not far from our town, running a racing-stable, manipulating millions of money, in the brief bright hey-day before he and our city came together upon a bleak and sober awakening.

*   *   *

All this was for the future, which was soon to throw wide its fiery doors. But now what we were living in was the end of an age that had lasted a long time. Edward might be on the throne, and in his own circle no doubt there had been a sweeping away of old pieties ; but in the country, and in our congregation as strongly as anywhere, Victoria still stood like a ghost at his elbow and Albert's photograph was on the mantelpiece. Throughout all the provinces of Britain, the Victorian Age lasted until the Great War.

It was upon a congregation of representatives of that age that I looked down from my seat in the front row of the gallery. The pew rents which periodically were " now due " were gathered only for seats in the body of the church. The gallery was free. Sitting there, I was now alone, for my elder brother, who was my great friend, I may almost say the only friend of my youth, was no longer with me. We were both at a stage of life when religious questions were troubling us, and troubling him, I imagine, more than me. We had both tired of the dreary repulsive atmosphere of the Brethren's chapel, but he did not accompany me to the Wesleyans because he firmly believed that baptism by immersion was in accordance with the will of God. But I recall with pleasure the sensible remark he made later : " I don't think all that matters."

He did not live long. He died of consumption in the flower of his youth. It was arranged by some who were then able to help us that he should take a voyage in a merchant ship for the good of his health. I alone accompanied him to the Cardiff docks when he embarked, and I recall how we stumbled about unaccustomed ways, in the dusk of the evening, stepping over hawsers, passing under the shadows of warehouses, till we found the ship. We were young and poor, timid and nervous and unused to life, and so, much as I should have liked to do so, I did not go aboard the ship to see his quarters. There seemed to be no one about in that quiet evening hour, and I stood there on the lip of the dock against which the ship lay for a long time. Then he came, alone, and leaned over the rail, and we talked of this and that, anything to fill the appalling moment, till he said : " Wait a minute " and disappeared again. I waited for many minutes, till the dark was fully come, and I could not screw up my courage to go aboard and say good-bye. And so that was the last I saw of him, leaning there over the dark rail, for he died on that voyage ; and I have often pictured to my mind the moment in the cabin whither he had retreated in order to screw up his

mind for a last farewell, and then could not bring himself
to come back and utter it. For some men, I think, know
when their doom is written. So it was with my younger
brother. We were both at home on leave in 1917, and his
leave was up before mine. On a winter's day in the opening of that year I went to see him off at the Midland station
in Bradford. We shook hands at the barrier, and I stood
there watching him walk along the train, with cap on his
head, the khaki overcoat collar upturned about his ears, the
clattering lumber of the infantryman hanging upon him at
all points. I hoped he would look back and wave to me,
as he trudged farther and farther with what seemed to my
eye a dedicated look, but I knew that he would not, that
here was being reenacted a moment I had lived through before. He got into a compartment right forward where the
huge glassy arc of the station's mouth was cut upon the
leaden light of that winter's day; and I went away knowing of a certainty that we had said good-bye for ever. We
had been five boys, though two I had never known. Now
I should be alone. A few months later, when I was back
in France, I learned that he had fallen at Arras.

*   *   *

Let us imagine that it is a summer evening as I sit in the
front row of the gallery. The chapel is cruciform, with
pews in the long arm of the cross and in the two short
arms. At the point where the arms meet stands the pulpit : a beautiful pulpit of white shining stone. Below it

in a semi-circle is the sweep of the polished communion rail. In front of the rail is a step, cushioned in red to ease the knees of communicants. Within the railed space is a red carpet and a small gothic-looking table. Behind the pulpit, on a level with the gallery, are the choir's seats, sloping up and back to the organ : that dreadful music-making instrument that caused the Brethren to shudder with horror and now, as the empty church begins to fill, causes me to shudder with delight. The congregation is assembling. The men carry tall silk hats in kid-gloved hands ; they wear frock-coats with satin lapels and striped trousers. It is a Sunday uniform that permits no deviation. The women are more varied. They wear crackling silk, full-skirted, or, especially the younger ones, a softer and more supple silk that accompanies them with a whisper and susurration. All, young and old alike, are *clothed* in the fullest sense of the word. They are covered all over, from the top of the neck down to the feet, and even beyond the feet, for, to walk comfortably, they hold their skirts clear of the floor with gloved hands. Seating themselves in the pews, they bend forward to pray. They do not kneel, for, though this is not the Brethren's chapel, neither is it an Anglican church. There are infinite gradations in these matters. The members of our congregation lean forward, rest their elbows on the book-ledge in front of the pew, and drop their faces into their hands, remaining thus, whether in prayer or mere conformity, for a few moments.

The pews are comfortable. Most of them have little

boxes to hold hymn-books and Bibles. They have cushions on the seats and hassocks on the carpeted floor. And they are well-filled. The steep fall-away in church attendance had not yet shown itself—in our chapel at all events. There is hardly a vacant space to be seen down there as the clock moves towards 6.30, when the service will begin. But there is a matter whose significance does not strike me as I lean on the gallery rail and look down into the body of the church. Here about me in the free seats are many empty places. Indeed, except on occasions of high excitement, such as the Chapel or Sunday School Anniversary, when not only will every seat in the gallery be filled, but people will be sitting on the steps there and, down in the body of the chapel, chairs will be placed in the gangways between the pews : except on such occasions as these, the gallery attendance will always be sparse and scattered. And the significance of this is, as I now see it, that the evangelistic fervour is gone. There is no contagion to infect strangers, no magnetism to draw them in. I was a member of the congregation for ten years or so, and in that time the congregational hierarchy did not change. There were no accessions, but a slight fading away at the older and younger ends. This bright and coloured and mainly well-to-do array on the floor of the chapel is at the end of a chapter. These are the families that have been nurtured in the habit and tradition of Methodism. Already, the younger members (as I began presently to discover) are becoming restless. Religious attachments are not strong

144

enough to hold them. They want more than "class-meet-ings" and "love feasts". There is a demand for a church sports-field and for plays in the Sunday School buildings, and these things will come, and prove as worthless in hold-ing young people to the Church as one might expect.

Well, there our congregation is, its private prayers said, on this summer evening like so many summer evenings I was to enjoy in that place. And the word *enjoy* is the word I want. Unlike the children down there in the pews, who may or may not be enjoying this occasion, I have not been brought to chapel; no one would question my doings if I were in some other church or chapel, or if I were out in the fields. I am here, all alone, because I want to be here, and I am enjoying myself.

The word has become debased : it has come to suggest anything but the sense of giving oneself Joy. Among its definitions of Joy, the Shorter Oxford Dictionary includes "exultation of spirit", and this is the precise sense in which I use the word here.

There were two main elements in this exultation. One was the music. I remember that the name of our volun-tary organist was Mr. Arthur Hutchings (another example, you see, of the West Country name in our town), and whether Mr. Arthur Hutchings was the inspired musician I then took him to be I shall never know. But I am free to presume that this well-to-do congregation, which liked to have everything of the best, would have an organ of the best, and indeed it seemed to me then that there could be

none better, either of organ or organist. Ignorant, in the
most complete and final sense, of music, I was easy prey for
all the tricks of which the organ is capable : the quavering
skyey notes that were like young lambs at play and the
belly-stirring rumble of the *vox humana*. I those days I
gave myself to Mr. Arthur Hutchings as freely and fully as,
to-day, I give myself to a Beethoven concerto played by my
gramophone. I have not the least desire to know what it
" means " any more than I wish to know the " meaning " of
the new moon and evening star. I abhor, and never read,
the explanatory programmes that the gramophone company
obligingly slips in with the records. Once, in my green
youth, a mamma, after a polite afternoon tea, asked her
daughter to play for us upon the piano. And as the daughter played, mamma drew a chair alongside mine and gave
me a whispered commentary on her prodigy's performance.
There came a run of trotting notes, and she explained, in
her conspiratorial hiss, " Ponies ! " and later, when these
notes recurred, " More ponies ! " Perhaps from that
moment dates by abhorrence of the " more ponies " school
of musical exposition.

Anyway, I was prepared to give myself as emotional clay
into the hands of Mr. Arthur Hutchings as his music soared
and vibrated under the lofty ceiling while our congregation
assembled, and again as they dispersed when the service
was ended. And during the service there was the marrying
of this music to the hymns we sang. In those hymns was
the second element of my joy.

I could write a lot about the Wesleyan hymn-book. During the time I was a member of the congregation the book was changed. I still have my copy of the new book I bought then, or rather that my brother bought, for it is his signature that is on the fly-leaf. But, as I have explained, he did not long remain with the Wesleyans but went to the Baptists, bequeathing his book to me. The Preface to this new book begins : " The present Hymn-book, ' for the use of the people called Methodists ', is the lineal descendant, after the lapse of one hundred and twenty-five years, of the volume so long known as ' Wesley's Hymns ', for which John Wesley wrote a celebrated Preface in 1779." This new book is dated " London, June 1904 ", and this helps me with my dates, because it tells me that I was fifteen years old when the book was published. As I had been a member of our congregation for some years, I would be twelve or thirteen years old when I began to attend the Wesleyan chapel.

It is this new book, not the old one which I must have handled for a few years, that is intimately bound up with my life at that time. I have it here on my desk before me, and it throws a flood of light into the backward abysm. It tells me a lot about my own infant mind. It tells me that, as I sat perched up there in the gallery, my thought must often have wandered from the sermon and engaged itself with its own affairs. The hymn-book was all I had to write in, and so I wrote in it. I find I have scribbled down a longish passage from Tennyson's " Holy Grail ", another from "In Memoriam", and the opening lines of Milton's "Ode to St. Cecilia"—

> Blest pair of sirens, pledges of heavenly joy,
> Sphere-born harmonious sisters, voice and verse—

which clearly reflected my feelings about Mr. Arthur Hutchings's playing and the singing of the hymns. There is also an appalling drawing of a human head, evidently a shot at a parson in the pulpit, which shows that then, as now, I could not put two congruous strokes together.

But sometimes my attention would be held, for I have scribbled what are evidently phrases that struck me out of sermons. "Worry is born of littleness." "God to an unholy man is Hell." And I must have been attracted from the beginning by that parson of whom I have said that he became a lifelong friend. He had then just come down from Oxford (not many Wesleyan parsons went there) and was given a church on our "circuit". In the hymnbook I have recorded (though I had forgotten this till I took it up a moment ago) the first text he preached from and the first hymn he gave out. He would be amused to know of this small piece of evidence that my young mind and his older one "clicked" from the beginning. But he will never know now. He went to Australia to be Principal of a training college, and died there.

But all this is the palimpsest imposed by myself upon the book. There remains the book itself. At the end of it is a "Biographical Index", giving the names of the hymn-

148

writers and a line or two about each. Now this biographical index became a factor of importance in my life. At
the Plymouth Brethren chapel we had used a book called
" Joy-bells ", or some such thing, containing little but the
jargon of hymnology.

> The Gospel bells are ringing
> Over land from sea to sea,
> Blessed news of free salvation
> Do they offer you and me.

That was the sort of thing : that was the emotional and
religious level they reached. I remember only one hymn in
that collection that stirred and moved me, and that was Dr.
Watts's " When I survey the wondrous cross ".

This is the hymn that stuck in young Arnold Bennett's
mind out of his chapel-going youth. In *Clayhanger*, as
Edwin Clayhanger and Hilda Lessways are watching the
great open air religious assembly, there is this passage :

And the multitude, led by the brazen instruments,
which in a moment it overpowered, was singing to a
solemn air—

> When I survey the wondrous cross
> On which the Prince of Glory died,
> My richest gain I count but loss,
> And pour contempt on all my pride.

Hilda shook her head.

" What's the matter ? " he asked, leaning towards her
from his barrel.

"That's the most splendid religious verse ever written!" she said passionately. "You can say what you like. It's worth believing anything if you can sing words like that and mean them!"

She had an air of restrained fury.

But fancy exciting herself over a hymn!

"Yes, it is fine, that is!" he agreed.

"Do you know who wrote it?" she demanded menacingly.

"I'm afraid I don't remember," he said. The hymn was one of his earliest recollections, but it had never occurred to him to be curious as to its authorship.

Her lips sneered. "Dr. Watts, of course!" she snapped.

It had never occurred to me to be curious as to the authorship of hymns until the Wesleyan book, with its biographical index, came into my hands. And now it came over me with the effect of a burst of light that we were worshipping in words written by men and women who were, to me, as gods. I cannot hope to convey to anyone who has not himself experienced something of the same sort the sense of almost maniacal devotion with which I cherished the names of poets and novelists and essayists. And here they were in this biographical index! Here was Kirke White, the story of whose sad brief days I had read, and Tennyson in whom I was steeped to the ears, and Sir Walter Scott, and Milton whose works had been handed on to me by my father. Here was Oliver Wendell Holmes, whose *Poet, Professor and Autocrat* were in three blue volumes on my shelves at home, and Anne Brontë, Christina Rossetti and Cowper, Addison, Whittier, Kingsley and Ellen Thorneycroft Fowler, whom I was, strangely enough, aware of as the contemporary author of a novel called *Concerning Isabel Carnaby*. It is no exaggeration to say that there was something almost in the nature of revelation here, bearing in mind my mental and emotional disposition at the time. If God was worshipped by these superlative beings, then indeed God was worshipful!

But there was even more than this to be discovered from the Biographical Index. It was packed with meagre but exciting hints of drama. "Newton, John (1725-1807)" it said. "Master of a slave ship. Became Curate of Olney. Friend of Cowper." How one could dream away a dull sermon in allowing the mind to embroider those few notes! Or there was this : "Newman, John Henry, D.D. (1801-1890) ; joined Church of Rome, 1845 : created Cardinal, 1879. 'Lead, kindly Light' written June 16, 1833, when orange-boat, in which he was sailing from Marseilles, was becalmed in Straits of Bonifacio." The orange-boat . . . the calm . . . the Straits of Bonifacio . . . ! What matter for dreams!

And there were hints of great happenings. "Luther, Martin (1483-1546) ; burnt Papal Bull 1520 ; attended Diet of Worms 1521." Evidently this excited some thoughts which it did not satisfy, for alongside it I see the word written in shorthand "Research", though whether that research was ever made I do not remember. The very names of some of the writers had an intrinsic excitement. Count von Zinzendorf; Anatolius (circa 800), "Greek hymn-writer and pupil of Theodore of the Stadium" (what could that be?); St. Bernard of Clairvaux; John Byrom, who was "the inventor of a system of shorthand"; and Johann Anastasius Freylinghausen, "Franke's colleague and successor at the Halle Orphanage". (Who was Franke? And who were these orphans at Halle?) Or there was St. Joseph the Hymnographer, "a slave in Crete". Slaves and masters of slave-ships, saints and shorthand writers, poets, novelists, essayists, and people distinguished by a swift tragic end, like Monsell "killed during the rebuilding of the church at Guildford". (Did he fall from a scaffolding? Did a great stone hurtle down and beat out his brains?) : these snippets (why was St. Theodulph "imprisoned in the cloister at Angers"?) filled the whole background of our worship for me, with a sense I had never had before of the "cloud of witnesses", the long, unbroken procession of faith and testimony.

So on this summer evening, when our congregation has settled its rustling silks, and Mr. Arthur Hutchings has ceased to play his opening music, and a steward has popped out of a door near the pulpit, leading from the vestry, and has placed a Bible and the day's announcements on the pulpit ledge, and the preacher himself has soon after followed, mounted the steps, and given out the opening hymn, you may be sure that the first thing I shall do is to turn to the index and see who is the author of this hymn, in what company we shall open our worship to-night. It is strange to me that no one else bothers to do this, or that the preacher does not say: "Let us sing Hymn No. 21, by John Milton" or "Hymn No. 118 by John Greenleaf Whittier"; for, when it comes to the text, he will tell us who wrote that; and, what is stranger, you will see down there in the body of the church all the Bibles opening, so as to verify that indeed there in the place named are the words mentioned. This is something they don't need to do, for the preacher has told them; but he has not told them whose hymn they are singing.

So the service proceeds, and, nine times in ten, what I shall most enjoy is the hymns and the music. The mixed choir of men and women seems to my uninstructed ear to be good, capable of moving harmonies, the tunes have a fine congregational swing, and the words a nobility far removed from the tinkling jingle of "Joy-bells".

> Join all the glorious names
> Of wisdom, love and power

(Dr. Watts again), or

> Holy, holy, holy,
> Lord God Almighty

have a power and strength that my young mind finds sustaining.

How many times, morning and evening, I took my joy in the gallery of the Wesleyan chapel? You were no one much so long as you sat in the gallery ; and I recall how, when a new, small chapel was built in the circuit, a boy whose privilege it was to sit in the body of the church suggested to me that I should betake myself there as it had been built " for the poorer people ". It was not so, of course ; yet I sometimes wonder what gossip at home—some half-expressed hope ?—may have prompted his tongue. For our congregation was very, very comfortable, removed, I have no doubt, by a moral league or two from what John Wesley would have considered a wholesome collection of " the people called Methodists ". It was the chapel of the Superintendent Minister of the circuit, a minor Cathedral of Methodism, a lotus-land where no harsh winds blew ; in a word, it was damnably comfortable.

I can recall but one occasion when passion shook the congregation. Our municipal elections were in prospect, and at a Sunday morning service a young and innocent parson was so ill-advised as to speak of them. Advocating no particular cause, he suggested that a vote could be cast, and should be cast, with a sense of religious responsibility.

A congregation is always quiet ; but, as soon as these words were out, one became aware of a new quality in the silence. The air was charged with outrage. An impious hand had swept into one heap the things of God and Caeser. Politics had been introduced into the Church !

The moment of suspense ended. With a freezing dignity, a member of the congregation took up his tall silk

154

hat and moved towards the door. Others followed. There they went, unhurried, nursing their silk hats and the kid gloves therein—walking out ! A symbolic moment ! The men of property, the men in good gets, walking out of the House of God! For so, one must presume, it was to them.

I was at that time a messenger boy in the office of one of our local newspapers, and here was News. I wrote my paragraph and that evening walked to the office and handed it in. The few lines obscurely appeared ; but they were notable lines to me : the first lines of mine ever to see print.

Many years were to pass before history made its comment on that dramatic moment in our chapel. Who could imagine that my friend the Fiery Serpent would be the instrument chosen to speak history's word ? But so it was. The war—World War I—had come and gone ; the Boom had followed, blazing the Fiery Serpent's trail comet-like across the sky ; and then, in a sputter of futile sparks, he was down to earth with the ruined ones who had put their faith in him. I have not much sympathy with those ruined ones. After all, what they are seeking is more and more for less and less : higher interest on money, and a fool's credulity in listening to the enchanters who promise it. But it happened that, being back on a visit to our city in those days, I was discussing the bleak scene with an old friend, and he said : " I could screw that man's neck, if only because —— —— lost all she had through him."

The words flashed my mind back to that Sunday morning so long ago, when war and booms and ruin were things not thought of, when the horse-trams were still jingling through our streets, and the Age of Gold was dreaming in its placid sunset. I saw the upstanding of the first of the outraged ones. I saw him taking up his hat and walking out, and I remembered that he was the father of this woman who now, in middle age, was one of the scattered bits of *débris* lying along the track of the Fiery Serpent. "The fathers have eaten sour grapes, and the children's teeth are set on edge."

Aha! I thought. Possibly that young parson was right, sir, and you were wrong. Possibly religion is, after all, something more than "glory for me". Possibly there is a link somewhere, hitching it up with justice for Tom, Dick and Harry, and I should like to know what justice there is, man's justice or God's justice, in money for nothing, which means goods for nothing, which means the labour of other men and women for nothing. Screwing higher and higher exactions for your paltry loans : is this the way of love ? Is this loving thy neighbour as thyself ? Is it certain that there are things of Caesar and things of God, with a comfortable smoke-screen of commercial convention and "business morality" in between ? Isn't it a fact that we shall have no rest, no peace, till the affairs of Caesar are done in the name and spirit of God ? Are not "the things of Caesar" a convenient cover for any sort of conduct on six days of the week, and "the things of God" a one-day wallowing in forgetfulness that God is the Father of us all ?

I felt as though I had seen Eternal Justice bring a wheel full circle. That young parson had had to apologise for dragging politics into religion ; and now here was an unapologetic God dragging religion into politics.

*   *   *

I am impelled into a digression. And not, you will say, for the first time. I shall digress on the subject of interest on money. My mind has not many obstinate obsessions, but this is one on which I am as obstinate as a mule.

Just before this war broke out, I was talking to a man who is friendly with a novelist so famous as to be known to us all. His earnings are enviable. My friend had just been to see him. The novelist complained that, though he was doing well and was able to have just about everything he wanted, "It's not good enough, because it all comes out of earnings."

What he wanted was to have so much money that, when it was invested, it would not matter whether he went on working or not. The invested money would keep him.

But would it ? Can a row of figures in a banker's ledger keep anybody ? Manifestly not. But investors don't realise this, or pretend that they don't. They don't face the fact that other people's sweat is keeping them.

I knew a man whose income before the war was about
a thousand pounds a year. He once told me how he came
to be in possession of this comfortable sum without working. He was a sailing man, and some time after the last
war he met a stranger during a regatta. They got on well
together, and one day this newcomer, who was in "big
business", dropped a hint that his firm and several others
were about to combine to control a large part of an essential
industry. "Put every penny you've got into it," he said.
My friend did so, and never worked again.

Here is another instance. I was reading the history of a
great industrial firm. It was one of those cases where, in
the beginning, both faith and cash were necessary. It
turned out marvellously well, and it dominates the world in
its own line to-day. Figures were given of the sums contributed by the early investors and what they mean to-day.
They are astounding. The return has not been ten-fold
but tens of thousand-fold. *And it is going on.* That is
the point.

When I am asked how much a man should have a
year, I say as much as he can earn. I don't care if it's ten
thousand a year so long as he earns it by labour that harms
no one. But to live on the return of investments made perhaps two, three, four generations ago—this revolts me.

In Mr. Sidney Dark's book *If Christ Came to London* I
read : "To-day the descendents of Charles Dickens do not
receive a penny piece from the sales of his novels. But if
Dickens, instead of making the world his debtor by writing

The Pickwick Papers, had founded a shoe factory or built houses sufficiently solid to have stood the test of time, his descendents would still be cashing in on the Dickens shoe or receiving rents from Dickens Terrace."

It is an illustration that makes you think. To carry it further : if, while Dickens was still writing, an investor had put his money into a publishing firm which continued prosperously till our own day, why, then his descendents would still be drawing dividends, while the descendents of the writers who alone made the publishing-house possible would be receiving nothing.

The Act of Parliament which governs the length of time during which a writer's descendents may draw royalties from his books takes into account that there comes a moment when a work of the imagination should be given freely to the world. It is right that this should be so ; and it seems to me that in the same way there comes a time when money, too, has received all that it has a right to expect and when the earnings of its beneficence should pass into a common pool. A man who lends money has a right to a return upon his loan ; but I see no case for saying that the return should go on and on through unpredictable generations. There could be much argument as to the moment at which the commonwealth should extinguish the claim of the individual, but until agreement is reached, and a position of equity is established between the state and the individual, I for one abhor and shun the whole business of putting money out at interest. With one exception, I live on what I earn, and when that evaporates I have to earn a bit more.

Perhaps we shall, before long, be *compelled* to invest, whether we want to or not. I see that the Government of Iceland has been elaborating a scheme for industrial expansion after the war. A lot of money will be needed, and one of the methods suggested for raising it is *compulsory* government bonds. So the rich of Iceland will be compelled to accept the fruits of other men's labour. In our own country during this war the propaganda in favour of National Savings of one sort and another has amounted to a psychological compulsion to invest. This constitutes in my own case the exception I have referred to. The government has so clamoured and dizzied our heads that I have lent what money I could. At any rate I have the consolation of knowing that taxation will see to it that I pay more than my own small interest on this money. This apart, I have no investments.

I once wrote an article dealing with these points, and a lady sent me a letter reproving me and telling me that obviously I was one of those who would end by living on the State's doles.

The letter is a good instance of the thick-headedness of those who uphold the present system. If I am to be kept, no " State " can keep me. I must be kept by myself or by other men and women. And what are these " doles " ? I cannot live on slips of paper passed over a Post Office counter, or even on these translated into pieces of copper and silver. Clearly, I must live on things to eat and drink, and things to use, made by other people. And this is what my letter-writer, if she is an investor, is doing all the time. The difference between us is that I shall do it as little as possible, and with luck, shall not do it at all.

To be of "independent means" was the passionate aspiration of thousands, and, I fear, still is. The ambition is admirable only if the "means" accumulated to make a man "independent" are his own earnings. I forget which of Mr. Galsworthy's Forsytes it was who told a young relation that the only thing in life that mattered was independence, and by that, of course, he meant having "independent means", that is, an income which makes a man independent not of work, but of working.

We must observe this distinction well, for no one can be independent of work. What the independent income ensures is that someone else shall do the work for you— every bit of the work : feeding, clothing, housing, lighting, heating. You can come and go as you please. There will always be someone to drive the car and the train. And when you get there, you will still find all the service you have left behind. You are an "independent" being, answerable to no one, but every non-Forsyte is answerable to you for work and service.

It is strange to find how many people who are in this position are cut to the heart by any proposal which threatens the "independence" of working people. Their letters flood the newspapers when such matters as the Beveridge

Report are in dispute. Above all things, they say, do not let us destroy the independence of the working man. For Forsytes, independence consists in having a lot without working for it, and this does not blind them to the mystical truth that for a working man independence consists in having a little by the sweat of his brow. For them, to be independent is to have things done for them; for a worker, to be independent is to retain the glorious freedom of for ever doing enough to keep body and soul together, plus the extra effort which earns the Forsyte dividends.

If relief from the more pressing of life's anxieties, the possession of two shillings to rub together, the knowledge that one can be put under the ground without an undue strain on relatives' purses : if these things are a sapping of independence, then it is time the Forsytes woke up and asked themselves whether they are independent beings after all. You can't call yourself "independent" because you've got money and then argue that a working man is only independent so long as he's got none. At least, you can't unless you are a Forsyte. I doubt whether all these State schemes will bring either heaven or happiness to earth. But that is another matter. All I am pointing out here is that what the Forsytes have to say about the threat to the "independence" of the working man makes me sick.

"How I hate money-lenders!" a Forsyte lady once said to me. Politeness forbad the reply : "Dear madam, you live by being nothing else!"

* * *

This is a Forsyte civilisation : it lives on money-lending. In rock-bottom terms, the " capitalist " is a money-lender : nothing else. The whole structure of the modern economic world is based on money-lending, money-borrowing, and the paying of interest. Most of us are up to the neck in all three. Our investments make us lenders, and, whether we wish to be so or not, we are borrowers and interest-payers through our citizenship. The municipality within which we live borrows on our behalf and we help to meet the bill when we pay our rates ; and so, too, with national taxation. All the nations of the world are living on taking in one another's debts. That, fundamentally, is what capitalism means.

The most violent anti-capitalists, those who spout most vehemently against the system, are often themselves involved in some phase or other of modern money-lending. Some simply do not realise that they are condoning the thing they denounce ; others, like Mr. Bernard Shaw, say that capitalism is abominable, but that, so long as it is there, we must support it.

This point of view is advanced and defended by Mr. Shaw in *Everybody's Political What's What ?* and it is interesting to compare his attitude in that book to religion and capitalism. I find the attitude inconsistent.

" Society," Mr. Shaw rightly says, " cannot be held together without religion," and it is equally incontestable that it cannot be held together without a political system. Our political system is capitalism ; our religious system, to use Mr. Shaw's words, is " anthropomorphic Deism ".

Mr. Shaw dislikes both these systems. He would like to see capitalism replaced by Communism and anthropomorphic Deism by Creative Evolution. Let him give his own account of Creative Evolution : " As I see the world, the statesman must be religious ; but he must discard every element in his religion that is not universal. He may have a vision of the whole human race bound together in a world-wide Catholic Church ; but he must not be either an Anglican Catholic or a Roman Catholic. If he personifies the creative factor in biology as God, he must not nationalise it as Jehova or Allah, Buddha or Brahma. Above all, he must not look to God to do his work for him. He must regard himself as the fallible servant of a fallible God, acting for God and thinking for God, because God, being unable to effect His purposes without hands or brains, has made us evolve our hands and brains to act and think for Him : in short, we are not in the hands of God ; but God is in our hands. A ruler must not say helplessly ' Thy will be done ' : he must divine it, find out how to do it, and have it done. His God must not be an existing Omnipotent Omniscient Perfection, but as yet only an ideal towards which creative evolution is striving, with mankind merely its best attempt so far, and a very unsatisfactory one at that, liable to be replaced at any moment if creative evolution gives it up as hopeless."

That is Mr. Shaw's religion ; but he concedes that " anthropomorphic Deism " will remain for long as a working hypothesis, not only for children but for many adults.

"Prayer consoles, heals, builds the soul in us; and to enact a Prohibition of Prayer, as some Secularists would, if they had the power, would be as futile as it would be cruel."

Believing then that what he holds to be a mistaken view of religion is better than no religion at all, and conceding that this system should be kept in being for those who want it until a universal acceptance of creative evolution comes along, Mr. Shaw nowhere tells us that he is prepared by, say, regular attendance at an Anglican church, to help to keep the mistaken but temporarily useful thing in being. When we come to his consideration of capitalism, we find his attitude is different. He thinks it is wrongheaded as "anthropomorphic Deism"; he wants to see it rooted out of the earth; but he warns us (and rightly) against rooting things out till we have something ready to put in their place, and he is prepared not only himself to worship at this unworthy shrine but to urge others to do so too.

He reminds us of Ruskin's saying that there are only three ways by which a man can live : by working, begging or stealing; and he leaves us in no doubt that he considers rents and incomes from investments to come under the third of these heads. Nevertheless, he tells us of his own profitable dealings on the Stock Exchange and says : "It is a demonstrable truth that in a capitalistic system the wisest practicable economic advice to the rich is : 'Invest all thou canst spare at the highest rate of interest compatible with reasonable security.'"

If it is a " demonstrable truth " that we should conform
to the general pattern of behaviour about us, even when
we think it mistaken, there arc several things to be said.
One is that this should be as reasonably applied to religious
conformity as to financial conformity and that Mr. Shaw
should therefore at once become a vicar's warden ; another
is that the acceptance of this " demonstrable truth " would
make nonsense of nearly all Mr. Shaw's books, which is a
series of calls *not* to conform to the accepted patterns in education, economics, in the attitude to medicine, war, and
what not.   But the most serious thing to be said about it is
that it cuts from under Mr. Shaw's feet the ground of his
own religious position.   If, as he says, God is fallible, unable to act and think unless " our hands and brains act and
think for Him ", how, one may ask, can this creative force
get any further with its purposes if those who believe they
see a more excellent way refuse to act in accordance with
their seeing, but wait till all the world is ready to move forward with them ?   This, as I see it, is again the flaw in the
humanist as distinct from the religious attitude.   The
humanist would go forward in a series of broad movements
imposed from on high ; religion insists on the importance of
the individual life acting in all things in accordance with
its own finest insight.   As no general movement can be
stronger than the individuals that compose it, the root of
the matter seems to me to rest with the religious attitude.

To know what should be done is all very well, but it
does not get us far.   Nine men in ten are aware not only

166

of all sorts of imperfections in their conduct but also of what they could do to correct these imperfections. But they don't do it. Hence New Year resolutions remain a good joke, and " Blessed are ye if, knowing these things, *ye do them* " remains a hard saying. It is interesting to note Mr. Shaw's opinion that the ruler who divines God's will must " have it done ". However, the command is not to " have it done ", which is the " ideological " method, but to do it, which is the religious method.

What Mr. Shaw fears is clear enough, and that is some widespread precipitate action that might upset the whole applecart. He reminds us that during the first ten years after the revolution the Russian Government " made so many legislative and administrative mistakes that the survival of the Communist State and even of the Russian people still seems miraculous and providential ". That is something that should not be lost sight of ; but the widespread consequences of a government's actions—" having it done "—are one thing, and the personal conduct of men who feel that a point of honour is involved—" doing it "— is another. These, you may be sure, acting against what is called " their own best interests ", will never be strong enough in numbers to derange in one swoop the body politic ; but their dislike of capitalism gains enormously in value if backed by a refusal to accept the benefits of what they denounce. My own refusal to invest money will not cause a panic on the Stock Exchange or bring our financial structure crashing ; but it does give me such personal satis-

faction as there may be in realising that I earn my own
bread. If the immensely richer Mr. Shaw joined me in a
similar resolution, the Old Lady of Threadneedle Street
would not lose a moment of her placid smile nor the foundations of the State show so much as a hair-crack ; but on the
positive side, it would be easier to see how Mr. Shaw's
theories about creative evolution work out in practice. For
what is involved is more than a quibble about this theory or
that : it is the whole question of whether our belief in good
can, in fact, be put to practice in our daily lives. How far
are we to accept " the custom of the country " when conscience disapproves of it ? How far do we accept the German plea : " What could I do against the might of the
Nazi party?" St. Paul made no excuses for himself but
laid to his own charge : " When the blood of Stephen
Thy witness was shed, I also was *standing by and consent-
ing*."

I must add that I am not, like Mr. Shaw, an anti-
capitalist. A man, in my view, is entitled to lend money
and to have a return for his services. But the system has
become corrupt and pernicious. It has reached a point
where it is possible for generation after generation to live
on the community without contributing any real work in
return. It has reached the idiocy of allowing some even
to live on the interest of interest. What could be a useful
service, with a recognised point at which the service was
paid off once for all, has become a world-wide burden and
menace, and I for one will have nothing to do with it. Or,

weak-willed as I am, as little as Government cajolery permits.

*   *   *

I have spoken of the flaw in the humanist attitude, but
this, I trust, will not range me with those who rail against
what they call " mere humanism ". *Mere* indeed! Humanism has been a great and powerful force in the world, one
of the cherished and precious ingredients in the Western
tradition of civilisation, and the task before us is not to
abolish humanism but to discover how its vast potentialities
can be used for even greater good. But humanism has become the whipping-boy of many Christians who, seeing the
declining influence of the Christian Churches in the
world, would shift the burden of responsibility on to other
shoulders.

This attitude is illustrated in a book called *Pastor's
Psychology* by the Rev. Arthur W. Hopkinson. " The
twentieth century ", the author says, " has shown up mere
humanism as a hollow sham. The philosophy in which
most men trusted has failed them and left them bewildered and ill at ease."

But there is no evidence whatever that throughout the
twentieth (or the nineteenth century) " most men " trusted
in humanism. Most men trust in nothing. They have
neither religion nor philosophy, and the true humanist is
a man in a million, like the true Christian. Furthermore,
by what warrant does Mr. Hopkinson place all the blame

169

for our present position upon humanism, whether *mere* or not ? To make good that case, he would have to show that humanism alone was operating in the contemporary world, that Christianity and all other forces for good had stood aside, saying : "Well, now, let's see what mere humanism will make of the job." This is not so. Christianity, rightly, has abrogated nothing of its claim to be effective. The failure is a failure all round. The Christian as well as the humanist has reason to be "bewildered and ill at ease."

G. K. Chesterton, who did not think humanism adequate, was at least generous enough not to snub it as "mere". In his book on Browning he wrote : "The ideals of the men of that period appear to us very unattractive ; to them duty was a kind of chilly sentiment. But when we think what they did with those cold ideals, we can scarcely feel so superior. They uprooted the enormous upas of slavery, the tree that was literally as old as the race of man. They altered the whole face of Europe with their deductive fancies. We have ideals that are really better, ideals of passion, of mysticism, of a sense of the youth and adventurousness of the earth ; but it will be well for us if we achieve as much by our frenzy as they did by their delicacies. It scarcely seems as if we were as robust in our very robustness as they were robust in their sensibility."

It seems to me that the need of to-day is to find the sparking-plug by which the spirit—the *essence* as the French call it—of Christianity can set in action the motor of humanism. A religious man in the just sense of the word is something that *is*. We are entitled to have the gravest doubts about the religious pretences of anybody who does not convey to our senses this apprehension of his *being*. The humanist, on the other hand, is concerned with *doing* ; and I for one refuse to believe that he could have done so much without access to some reservoir of power, to something that anyone concerned with the good of the race must take into account. It is all very well for the disgruntled and disappointed Christian to say : "Yes; but for all his doing, look at the state of the world to-day." Well, look at the state of the world before humanism interposed, when Christianity was accepted as the one inspiration of the good life. Was man less greedy and vain, less of a liar, less itchy and trouble-stirring then than now ? Did he get along without war ?

Yes, you say, but look at the *horror* of modern war. Wars become more and more diabolical.

True. But did the humanist invent modern armaments ? War is to-day precisely what it always was : the use of the most diabolical instruments available at a given time. The *spirit* of the thing, which is what matters, is unchanged. Certainly there is no record of a Christian protest against the substitution of the rifle for the bow and arrow and the cannon for the battering-ram.

Christianity, as I see it, is in its present bedraggled condition because it has not found—or has lost—the sparking-plug that would transform its spiritual essence into human energy. When called upon to do so, it has too often taken up its top hat and walked out of church. Knowing these things is half the story; doing them is the other half; and either half is in itself a crippled thing. "Man does not live by bread alone, but by every word that proceedeth out of the mouth of God," and the more I look at that saying, the more startling is the emphasis with which the word *alone* stares out at me. It was not for nothing that Jesus, the master of parable and revealing allusion, decreed that men would come most aptly and deeply into the presence of God when they sat down together and shared their food and drink, seasoned with love.

No; the Christian who decries humanism is off on the wrong foot. This strange creature man is a two-horse shay dragged along the road of life by body as well as spirit. The two should be pulling as one, because the Word and the flesh are not separate things. The Word was made flesh, and this powerful but baffling amalgam is what we have to deal with; but the two are dizzied and pulled apart by the distracting counsels of religion and humanism, and so the cart is ditched and there is a whirr of hoofs threshing the barren air. Does not the General Epistle of St. James give us the word that binds them together? "Pure religion and undefiled before our God and Father is this: to visit the widows and fatherless in their affliction, and to keep himself unspotted from the world. . . . For as the body apart from the spirit is dead, even so faith apart from works is dead."

Archbishop Trench, in *English Past and Present*, reminds us that when our Bible was translated the word "religion" did not mean, as it means now, the "sum total of our duties towards God". It meant, he says, "like the Latin *religio*, the outward forms and embodiments in which the inward principle of piety clothed itself, the *external service* of God". He therefore warns us against deducing from the words of St. James which I have quoted that the writer considered good works to compose the whole duty of man towards God. But I don't think there is much need to carp and analyse here. St. James makes his position clear enough : faith *and* works ; works *and* faith ; the Word and the flesh ; the sparking-plug and the motor. Religion and humanism are not antithetical; they are complementary. They are the seed and the soil, the grist and the mill.

*　　　*　　　*

My recollection of how the men of property rose up in protest in our Wesleyan chapel on that Sunday morning so long ago has led me wide afield, and it is time to get back to the boy sitting there in the gallery. I want to have another look at his hymn-book, because, considering the biographical index as it lies here on the desk before me, I notice a point of interest. A mark has been made against many names, and this is puzzling, for the men and women so marked appear to have nothing much in common. Suddenly it comes over me that these marks, made forty or so years ago, were made precisely because there is so little in common between the people thus singled out.

Here, for example, we have St. Bernard, the twelfth-century Abbot of Clairvaux, Abélard's powerful opponent, and we have also a certain Frederick Lucien Hosmer, a nineteenth-century Unitarian minister of Massachusetts. Bernard wrote one of the loveliest of hymns : "Jesu, the very thought of Thee with sweetness fills my breast"; but this sweetness did not prevent him from declaring "The Christian exults in the death of a pagan, because Christ is glorified."

It would have been vain for Mr. Hosmer to say, as he does in his hymn :

> O Thou who are of all that is
> Beginning both and end,
> We follow Thee through unknown paths,
> Since all to Thee must tend.

Bernard, for all that, would have considered him a heretic, ripe for the fate that could and plentifully did overtake heretics in the twelfth century.

The markings indicate, too, Anglican bishops and vicars, a certain Mrs. Elizabeth Codner, briefly dismissed as "a worker at Mildmay Hall", whatever that may have been ; Wesleyan ministers, Congregational ministers, Baptist ministers ; plenty of Unitarians in addition to Mr. Hosmer ; Newman and F. W. Faber, who in their time were

first Anglicans and then Roman Catholics ; a schoolmaster,
a Moravian bishop, St. John of Damascus, " Father of the
Greek Church," a Sheffield manufacturer, a judge, a professor of theology, a seventeenth-century German Imperial
Counsellor, Mr. Albert Midlane, of whom it is simply
recorded that he was " in business at Newport, Isle of
Wight ", Edward Osler, " surgeon and editor ", a schoolmaster's wife who composed hymns " for the boys in Mr.
Owen's boarding-house ", a Leeds solicitor, a Lutheran
pastor, a " painter and essayist ", Thomas Sternhold,
Groom of the Robes to Henry VIII ; to say nothing of the
poets and novelists, slaves and slavers, who had already
caught my eye.

Here then, I began dimly to see, was something wider
than the naïve little discussion my brother and I used to
have as to whether baptism by immersion was in accordance with the will of God. Here, stretching back through
the centuries, was every sort of man and woman, sundered
by the deep divisions of creed and rite, many of whom
would have considered the rest in danger of hell fire; here
was something more than a cloud of witnesses : for here
were witnesses who would look with profound suspicion
upon one another's evidence ; not only a multitude of
voices uttering every conceivable note from the majesty
of the Gregorian chant to the cacophony of "Glory for
me ", but a multitude mutually wary and hostile. Yet
from all these sources this hymn-book had been gathered
together ; and these old stagers of Methodism down there,

who were not far from considering Catholicism as the Whore of Babylon and Unitarianism as scarcely a religion at all, would gladly sing the words of Bernard or Newman, Whittier and Wendell Holmes.

I was to find consolations in my Wesleyan chapel for many a year to come ; but I think from the time when the " inwardness " of that biographical index sank into my mind I was never again to be deeply disturbed by the catchwords of the sects.

To this day, when I find appeals going forth for the " unity of the churches " I wonder what it is that is wanted. I hope it is sufficiently borne in mind that unity and uniformity are different things. If it is, as I believe it is, implicit in the teaching of Jesus that the individual human being is the basis and bedrock of everything, then uniformity, the destructive dogma of contemporary polit-ical science, is to be avoided at all costs : even at the cost of disturbing much of the smooth and oily bureaucratic flow of existence that seems to-day a desirable ideal to so many. This is true both of our religious and political life. One vast church imposing its dogma upon us all would be a nightmare, and unity calls for nothing of the sort. A family is united, not uniform, and the quirks and idio-syncrasies of its members are the very cement of the union, the very blood of the covenant. For what covenant is necessary among identically-acting ciphers ? How shall the bass-viol and the flute find uniformity ? But in the harmony of a symphony they find unity because each supplies to the other what the other has not. Harmony is the consequence of due weight given to many factors, some of them opposites ; and peace is the consequence of harmony. Our breasts are filled with peace as we contemplate a harmonious landscape, composed as it may be of so many factors : the moving cloud against a moveless hill, the restless sea lapping the changeless rock. The harmony of the mind is wisdom : so different a thing from knowledge, which is restless and questing. Wisdom puts knowledge in its place alongside all that can never be known. It is of wisdom that the Proverbs say : " Her ways are ways of pleasantness and all her paths are peace."

It is worth nothing that these words are spoken of wisdom, the *harmonious* quality of the mind. It is harmony—that is, unity, not uniformity—which produces pleasantness and peace. But what have pleasantness, peace and harmony to do with our modern world, with charters, pacts, protocols, lend-lease, all the brouhaha, guff and gabble of social and political strife ? Everything. For it is literally true that if we seek first the Kingdom of God and His righteousness, which is the Kingdom of peace and harmony, all these things shall—not may, *shall*—be added unto us. We are putting the cart before the horse if we think that the Kingdom of heaven will come out of political understandings. The truth is that just political and all other understandings can only come out of the Kingdom of heaven. To the extent that these political motions are made in the spirit of brotherly love, and thus have behind them the force and sanction of a living breath, they will succeed ; to the extent that they are mere expediencies they will fail, for the living breath of love must both create and sustain them. It is that, not they, which is the prime mover : it can never be the other way about. And it is in the very nature of this love for one another that each shall recognise the right of the other to exist in the full terms of his own being, and indeed not only the right of this but its supreme *value* to us all. But this will hardly be apprehended by an idiot breed which, wanting bread, decides that the best way to get it is by charging in tanks across fields of ripening wheat.

*   *   *

Up in the ceiling of the chapel there were a few coronets of gas-burners, with a by-pass that allowed a glimmer of light always to exist there. As the summer passed into autumn, the light inside the building would be fading towards the end of the sermon, and in the gallery the chapel-keeper would appear with a long slender rod. Leaning over the rail, he would reach with this upward and outward, hooking the small rings which, being pulled, allowed the gas to flow freely into the burners. The windows, which had been fading to an ash-grey, would go black, and inside the chapel the service would move to its end in a glow of light. Mr. Arthur Hutchings at the organ would be giving us his moving accompaniment to our hymn :

> The day Thou gavest, Lord, is ended,
> The darkness falls at Thy behest.

It was one of my favourites. While we sang the words

> As o'er each continent and island
> The dawn leads on another day

my mind's eye would see the sun sinking away in the west
beyond the nose of Pembrokeshire, and Ireland swinging
up under it, and all the wide Atlantic to the American
shore. Then America would tilt down eastward under
the sun and a different sea come into sight : the sea of
Ballantyne's *Coral Island*, blue and luminous, tufted with
palms, and in the middle of that sea would be Australia.
A boy I had known casually had gone to live there, and to
me it seemed most moving to think of this sun, which now
was leaving us, in due time touching his eyelids and rous-
ing him to another day. I do not know why this should
have been so, but so it was.

I liked better those evenings of high summer when the
chapel-keeper and his rod did not appear, and the service
ended with the first dusk sliding into the chapel. In the
porch the free-seated inhabitants of the gallery could not
help mingling for a moment with the pew-renting top-
hatters from downstairs. There they were, putting on
their hats, drawing their kid gloves on carefully finger by
finger, a few wearing at their lapels the touch of blue
ribbon that meant total abstinence from liquor. (Do you
remember the phrase in Mr. Sherlock Holmes's adventure

of *The Cardboard Box*? " I was blue ribbon then, and we were putting a little money by.") This was the moment, this the spot, where parties were formed for the summer Sunday evening parade that was almost ritual. The chapel stood at the intersection of two streets, and one of these led to the open country. There were four or five splendid fields with a roadway through them, and beyond them was the tall spire of Llandaff Cathedral which stood on a green plate with the Taff meandering by, and with a hill rising steeply on its southern side. This hill was a spur of the last step down from the South Wales mountains on to the alluvial plain that was the site of our city. The village of Llandaff itself stood—and stands—on the hill, above the spire of its own cathedral, and in those days the 'bus which ran from our city to Llandaff needed a cockhorse to help it up the hill. It was just at the point where the cockhorse used to stand waiting for the 'bus that our chapel's Sunday evening parade entered the Llandaff fields. To be the boy in charge of the cockhorse, hitching him to the 'bus, urging him up the hill, and then jingling down again in freedom, seemed to me then a romantic and desirable office. But soon the cockhorse would go, and a few switches in our chapel would take the place of the chapel-keeper's laborious rod. We were, in all sorts of ways, though we knew it not, at the end of an age.

After many years of absence, I stood again, during this present war, on the hill of Llandaff, looking down at the cathedral below me. A large jagged stone lay at my feet, and, bending to examine it, I deciphered a few broken words of what evidently was a mortuary inscription. A bomb had fallen down there, damaging the cathedral, and the blast had shattered a tombstone and thrown this heavy fragment right up the hill to rest on its tip. Nothing had ever more clearly spoken to my heart of the passing of all that had once seemed inviolable. The young to-day, I imagine, can have no such sense as we had then of a pattern that appeared fixed and irrevocable. Here timeless innocent hours had passed over my head as I wandered among the tombstones, imagining this churchyard to be that of Gray's *Elegy*, murmuring those ageless rhymes, examining with a delicious shudder the grave-digger's shed where spades and boards and clay-toughened ropes were housed and where the charnel smell of an elderberry tree was bitter on the warm evening air; or, standing at the west door, inhibited somehow from entering, listening to an unseen organist filling the dark with music and unseen boys sending their voices up like birds in the darkness. Over the Taff, which murmured upon its pebbles the dusk would be deepening. The sky beyond the heavy mass of Garth mountain would be a last red smoulder, and the first bats would come to squeak among the last swallows. I do not know how it is now, but then the cathedral chimes would play hymn-tunes, and the memory of those notes dropping into the air about the water-meadows is a very part of my childhood and youth. The whole place is a-swarm with memories that are all happy but one. There was a deep narrow feeder drawn off from the river to serve a mill that once ground corn, and there the little wanton boys would bathe on summer evenings. I was walking along the feeder one night just at the moment when a body was dragged out of the water. They laid it on the bank, a small thin body, naked as nature, of a ghastly bluey-white; and as I stopped with a child's horrified fascination to gaze upon it I recognized a boy I knew. He had been my enemy in one of those childish feuds that arise who knows how? I would be hard put to it to say why he had made my life a misery, so far as he could, shouting and throwing stones; but so it had been; and now there he lay beyond all further power to do me harm: a plaster of wet hair, a miserably thin-looking white corpse. My enemy was dead, and all joy seemed to die out of the summer evening.

But on that day when I stood upon the hill of Llandaff and found a broken tombstone at my feet and looked upon the wounded cathedral, it was not of the dark but the bright enchantments of childhood that I was thinking. I was thinking of a pattern that had so long endured, and of the little thought that any of us, young or old, gave to the possibility of change. Around the cathedral, under the guttering, there were corbels of stone, and upon these the heads of the British kings and queens were carved with Cromwell thrown in as a generous democratic gesture. I forget how many of these bosses were left uncarved in my childhood—not many—and there was an old wives' tale that when there were no more, kingship would vanish from

England. Such speculations would entertain our minds, but only lightly, only as one might talk with amused disbelief of the predictions of soothsayers and wise women. No eyes were turned in the direction whence the storm in truth would come, wrenching apart what we took for immovable, and dissolving into a still unpredictable flux the outlines of our indissoluble pattern.

*   *   *

Did it ever rain in childhood ? Were summer days ever less than without end, glorious in the dawn and magical at nightfall ? I seem to remember nothing but a procession of perfection ; and certainly it is only of summer's best that I can think when I call back to memory the Sunday evening church parade through the fields of Llandaff.

There were our elders and betters in their tall hats and formal clothes, their women in whispering silk, their sons in straw hats and neatly-held kid gloves, parading in a slow solemn procession upon the grass which edged the roadway, grass that is remembered as always brown with summer's heat, thin-worn and slippery with the passage of many feet. There was a church not far from ours—Presbyterian, if I remember aright—which also was a haunt of the well-to-do ; and thence a tributary stream would meet our Wesleyan flow, and the two would move westward, to encounter presently the eastward-flowing stream from the Cathedral.

It was a picture of middle-class comfort and self-satis-

faction, sedate, and not without certain virtues of thrift
and solidity, poised upon the brink of dissolution. I recall
the women as wearing layer upon layer, like onions. The
arms would be clothed in kid gloves that reached to the
elbows. A hand would hold up the flounce of the long
trailing skirt ; and beneath this would be glimpsed further
garments of silk that, one had to suppose, were by no
means the end of the matter. All this, I could hardly be
expected to know, was the symbol of the inviolability of
women. The word "morality" was still used to mean
nothing but chastity in the unmarried and monogamy
among the married. Till marriage, a woman was a flower
set apart, not growing wildly upon a bush but exhibited
on the florist's counter, wrapped in sheet after sheet of
tissue-paper. The body—the woman herself—must, all
save the face, be concealed, and it was with this body that
"morality" was concerned. The chorus-girl of the time
was as voluminously clothed as this sedate sister walking
through the fields of Llandaff, and her daring consisted in
so dramatically flinging up the leg as to display not only a
length of black stocking but occasionally a bit of white
thigh above it. How deeply embedded was this idea of
"morality's" concern with the flesh, and especially the
flesh of a woman's leg, a sad happening showed during
one of those decorous Sunday evening parades through the
summer fields of Llandaff. Among these walkers was a
pair of lovers, indistinguishable from the rest in their re-
spectable uniform : he wearing his silk hat and frock coat,

she in swathe upon swathe of fragile silk. The young man lit a cigarette and threw the match to the ground. It fell, still burning, upon the flounces of the girl's skirt, and in a flash she was a pillar of fire. She died there in the field where she lay. I did not see this happen, but I knew the girl well, though she must have been ten years older than I was, and so the affair made a deep impression on my mind. I remember hearing it discussed, and this phrase is burned in my memory : "Till someone threw a coat over her, she was showing all she had." The words remained in my mind because to me too, so contagious is the "moral" outlook of one's moment, it seemed the last horror of that moment that this poor girl, lying there dead in the summer evening field, should be "showing all she had". That her young life should flame away like a sudden torch seemed a small matter compared with the shame of this.

*   *   *

John Wesley gave the "class meeting" a central place in the organisation of "the people called Methodists". It had a financial as well as a religious importance. The institution of these classes showed Wesley's skill in seizing upon a hint, for it was a word dropped with no thought of its large possibilities that led to the founding of the "classes". Southey, in his *Life of Wesley*, tells us that it came about thus :

When the meeting-house was built at Bristol, Wesley had made himself responsible for the expenses of the building : subscriptions and public collections had been made at the time, but they fell short. As the building, however, was for their public use, the Methodists at Bristol properly regarded the debt as public also; and Wesley was consulting with them concerning measures for discharging it, when one of the members proposed that every person in the society should contribute a penny a week till the whole was paid. It was observed that many of them were poor, and could not afford it. "Then", said the proposer, "put eleven of the poorest with me, and if they can give anything, well; I will call on them weekly; and if they can give nothing, I will give for them as well as for myself. And each of you call upon eleven of your neighbours weekly, receive what they give, and make up what is wanting." The contribution of class-money thus began, and the same accident led to a perfect system of inspection. In the course of their weekly calls the persons who had undertaken for a class, as these divisions were called, discovered some irregularities among those for whose contributions they were responsible, and reported it to Wesley. Immediately he saw the whole advantage that might be derived from such an arrangement. This was the very thing which he had long wanted to effect. He called together the leaders, and desired that each would make a particular inquiry into the behaviour of those under his care. "They did so," he says, "many disorderly walkers were detected; some turned from the evil of their ways; some were put away from us; many saw it with fear, and rejoiced unto God with reverence." A few weeks afterwards, as soon as Wesley arrived in London, he called together some of his leading disciples, and explained to them the great difficulty under which he had hitherto laboured of properly knowing the people who desired to be under his care. They agreed that there could be no better way to come at a sure and thorough knowledge of every individual than by dividing them into classes, under the direction of those who could be trusted, as had been done at Bristol. Thenceforth, whenever a society of Methodists was formed, this arrangement was followed : a scheme for which Wesley says he could never sufficiently praise God, its unspeakable usefulness having ever since been more and more manifest.

What has happened to the "class meeting" now that the Wesleyans are united in one church with other Methodists I do not know, but in my time it was still, theoretically, the core of Wesleyan Methodism. A person who was a "class member" was automatically a member of the Church. But though this was the theory, class membership had fallen to a low ebb. To any observant eye, two things "stuck out" where the classes were concerned. Few of the younger people attended them ; and they were a sorting of the people into social degrees. It was out of my own observation of the classes at that time that I wrote, much later, these lines in a novel called *Fame Is The Spur* :

"One by one, Gordon's class members assembled. They were all poor people. It was a gibe of Birley Artingstall's that Wesleyan 'classes' were like that. 'They're all graded, Gordon. You've got the nothing-a-weeks. Someone else has the pound-a-weeks, and so they go on. Anyone with more than five pounds a week doesn't bother to attend class at all, unless he happens to be a class leader.' "

That is how I found it. Our class met on Thursday nights in one of the rooms under the chapel, a room filled on summer evenings with delicious green wavering light. Our "leader" was a well-to-do business man, and our members were a handful of poor people. It was Wesley's intention that the class members should fortify one another by testifying to the power that belief exercised in their lives. This, in our class, had worn down to a thin and rather embarrassing convention. After our hymn-singing and Bible-reading, the leader would give us a short address, and then he would go round our small assembly asking each by name to testify.

"It was evidently a well-understood routine." (I quote again from *Fame Is The Spur*.) "Gordon's eye rested on the first woman in the back row of seats. She stumbled to her feet and recited in a gabble : 'Thank the Lord, Mr. Stansfield, and forget not all His benefits. I've felt the benefit of my religion all through this past week. I've needed the help of God, and I've had it.' "

So it would go. I cannot recall one occasion in a class meeting when the mind was smitten with the conviction : "There is someone talking out of the heart. There is someone having access to a source." It was all a cut-and-dried formality that gave the heart nothing.

*   *   *

While the class meetings thus dwindled to shadows, the " social life " of the church, as it was called, prospered mightily, but of this I can speak only from observation, not from participation. There was the Wesley Guild, an organisation worthy enough, wherein the members read papers to one another on literary and other matters and from time to time burst out into something called a " conversazione ". An occasional play was staged in the Sunday-school building, causing the elder members of the congregation to shake their heads over the desecration of " Trust premises ", and in some fields on the outskirts of the town there was provision for bowls, football and tennis. As I see it now, the problem evidently was how to keep the young people in the church ; and so these means were adopted. It was all as though a professor of philosophy should hope to keep his pupils true to Plato by providing them with facilties to read *Ally Sloper's Half Holiday*.

Who were in the rights of it—the Brethren who condemned plays and football and literature as works of the Devil, or the Wesleyans who provided all these things as accessories of the church ? Neither, I think. Of the frenzied wrong-headedness and wrong-heartedness of the Plymouth Brethren I shall say nothing more. As for the secular enterprises of the Wesleyans, it is enough to say that they have been condemned by their own failure. They have not kept up the numbers of the church members. That is not because they were wrong, but because they sought to attract to a mighty cause by trivial means.

189

That men in the church should have an opportunity to play football is sensible enough, but that young men playing football might thereby be tempted to give an occasional look-in at church: this was a great surrender of the dignity of worship. And things did seem to get that way round. A church which cannot win and keep its membership by its religious teaching alone is a defeated church, for all these accessories are better provided by those whose business it is to do them well. Look at that question which burned so many of the older members of our congregation : Should plays be permitted on Trust premises? The answer seems to me to be No : not because Trust premises are too good, but because they are not good enough. If I want to see a play, why watch juvenile Wesleyans amateurishly cavorting upon a few square yards of platform when we have in our city a few theatres where the job is properly done? There is one glory of the sun and another glory of the moon ; but the glory of a church is not to be measured by the acreage of its playing fields.

*　　　　*　　　　*

We had then the Sunday school, the various social activities, the class meetings, the common run of Sunday services, and the special occasions when some celebrated preacher of the denomination—perhaps even the august President of the Conference—would come to address us.

These occasions usually prolonged themselves from the Sunday into the Monday, when the wonderful visitor would wind up the exciting week-end with a lecture. There is one thing to be said about both these normal services and the special services, and it has been well said by Mr. Christopher Hollis in his book *Fossett's Memory*. He speaks there of the charge often made by Protestants against Roman Catholics that they deny themselves direct access to God and depend upon the intermediation of a priest. But he points out that the central fact of the Roman Catholic service is the Mass and that before this mystery all are as dust; whereas in a Protestant church (and, though Mr. Hollis does not make the point, this is especially true in a Nonconformist church) the central fact is a man preaching a sermon, a more obstinate interposition between the worshipper and the worshipped than you will find in any Catholic church.

Though I did not think so then, I think now that this is a point of importance; and in the unlikely event of my attaching myself again to a congregation, it would be to one which assembled rather to make an act of contrition and worship than to listen to a sermon.

A Wesleyan parson of those days preached at least two sermons a week, and though John Wesley had the sense and foresight to institute the system whereby his preachers moved to a new scene of labour every three years, and could therefore, if they felt so disposed, get along on, say, three hundred and fifty sermons : still, even to produce

191

so many as that supposes a spiritual dynamism that is not common. There are Nonconformist preachers who remain in one church for far longer than three years and succeed nevertheless in attracting and holding large congregations, but these are unusual men : men who *overflow*, so full they are, and it is to be doubted whether a general practice is wisely based on the example of exceptions.

My recollection is that the normal run of the sermons I listened to in those days was, as they say, " well enough ", and some of the " special occasion " sermons were notable ; but, taking the whole thing by and large, we listened to the commonplace thoughts of commonplace men, and, for me, the essence of the matter tended to be more and more in those parts of the service which were acts of worship : and these were the hymns and the holy communion.

I had first become acquainted with the communion service in the chapel of the Brethren, though I did not partake there. Sitting behind the notice which divided the unbelievers from the elect, I would watch the service go forward among those on the front benches. It was a wordless service, consisting of passing along a loaf of bread from which each participant tore a piece and ate it before handing the loaf on to his neighbour, and then similarly passing a flagon of wine which was sipped and circulated.

In the Wesleyan chapel the practice was different. First of all, those who did not wish to communicate left the building. Then we from the gallery came down into the body of the church and all gathered into the first few rows of pews. We were but a small number as a rule. Our organist was gone, and our hymn-singing was unaccompanied and somewhat quavering. Usually, we began with Dr. Bonar's

> Here, O my Lord, I see Thee face to face;
> Here would I touch and handle things unseen.

This is a hymn that always deeply moved me, especially the verse :

> Too soon we rise ; the symbols disappear ;
> The feast, though not the love, is past and gone ;
> The bread and wine remove, but Thou art here,
> Nearer than ever, still my shield and sun,

and a sense of the transience of life always powerfully visited me as we sang the last verse :

> Feast after feast thus comes and passes by . . .

The service went closely along the lines of the Anglican Book of Common Prayer. As we knelt on the red cushion that followed the semicircular sweep of the polished mahogany rail, the parson moved before us, holding out first a basket containing small cubes of bread, then a container furnished with glass thimbles of wine, murmuring as he went the well-known words of the service. When all had communicated, another hymn was sung, the parson pronounced the Benediction, and we went away. It was rare to see anyone attend this service who was not one of the old traditional Methodists or a son or daughter detained by the unuttered authority of a Methodist home. This was true also of the prayer-meetings which now and then, at no set time, apparently by the minister's whim, would follow an evening service. I attended many of them and got to know exactly which old stagers could be relied on to rise and utter their petitions. The very words of the petitions became in time familiar. These members of the Old Guard of Methodism—the last, I imagine, to conserve some flavour of Methodism as it was in Wesley's day—had carved their parentheses and perorations throughout so many years that they had but to start and off they would go, not " down the ringing grooves of change " but down accustomed by-ways of which they knew every landmark. Old Birley Artingstall's prayer in *Fame Is The Spur*, working up to a climax in which he calls upon the Lord to return and " sway the sceptre of universal dominion ", is from a model which I heard often rehearsed in those old days.

*   *   *

There happened, during this time when I was entering into my late teens, one of those strange phenomena known as religious revivals. There arose in Wales a man named Evan Roberts, and that name, I suppose, will never be forgotten as long as " revivals " remain a matter of interest and curiosity. Wales was shaken to the core. Wherever Evan Roberts went violent manifestations broke loose.

Men howled and sang and prayed and declared that they had given themselves to God. The old *cliché* which compares a fervid movement to a bush-fire was true enough in this case. The fervour swept the country. The Welsh newspapers gave columns of space every day to the remarkable scenes that were witnessed, and the national press could not but take extensive note of so unusual an affair. Cardiff itself was merely brushed by the skirts of the revival. Efforts were made to induce Evan Roberts to visit the city, but he did not do so. The mining valleys, where every village had its Horeb, Hebron and Ebenezer, were the scene of his chief work. I forget how long the delirium endured, but I know that it was for a considerable time. When the storm of emotion had blown itself out, Evan Roberts ceased to be of any note in the religious life of Wales. As bright as a meteor, as disturbing as an earthquake, he was as transient as either. What became of him I do not know. I saw nothing, though I read much, and because of the charged atmosphere was aware of much, of the things that happened about his person. The whole question of " revivalism " in religion is dark to me with a darkness that I distrust. The organised and almost commercial revivalism of missions such as that of Torrey and Alexander, moving with handbills and advertising agents like a circus from one part of the country to another : this is one thing ; as I see it, a thing of machinery. Whatever Evan Roberts's revival may have been, it was not mechanic : it was a thing of fire, frenzied and Dionysiac : a thing of personality : and once that personality had burnt itself to a cinder in the heat of its own possession, all was over.

Though I did not attend any of these meetings, it happens that I can give a first-hand account of the way in which *possession*—I think it is the only word to use—deals with the possessed. A few years later, when I was a young reporter on *The Yorkshire Observer*, a movement known as the Holiness Pentecostal Convention staged itself in Bradford. I was sent to write a description of the happenings, and the editor of *The Yorkshire Observer* has kindly given me permission to reproduce here what I wrote in April, 1914. I do so because it pleases me to consider again the way in which I used to write in my early reporting days, and because, I feel sure, the scenes here described are to an appreciable extent such as ravaged Wales in the days of Evan Roberts.

The strange manifestations of religious fervour that marked the opening of the Holiness Pentecostal Convention on Friday were repeated in the mission room in Bowland Street, Bradford, on Saturday. Both in the afternoon and evening unaccustomed waves of emotion swept over the worshippers, causing them to sing ecstatically, to moan as though in pain, to throw themselves prostrate as before a vision clear to them though dark to those about, to croon to themselves, or to break forth unaccountably into rapturous praises or mystic jargon.

Through the windows of the stuffy little room the sun shone upon the bare boards of the floor and the austere walls, unadorned save for the photograph of Evan Roberts

196

and a few scripture texts. Not a window was open, and the almost foetid atmosphere was thickened by the fumes from the little coke stove in the centre. On the hard forms sat a motley gathering. Here was a little Salvation Army lass who had hobbled in on tortured limbs. Seated at the rickety harmonium was a girl with an oval face of the Burne-Jones type, clear and spiritual, but with a too fragile intensity. A stout old woman with a small black bonnet pinned to her gathered hair gazed stolidly before her as though oblivious of all around; and at the other side of the room a white-haired, snowy-bearded old man trembled on his seat. There was a man with a great black shovel-beard and black hair, who looked as though he had stepped from Rothenstein's " Carrying the Law ", so set on one thought his mind seemed. There were many others—all of the middle class.

Their minds were fixed with one accord on a central purpose which was voiced again and again as "the Power". They implored it in hymns, whose garishness was counterbalanced by the intensity of their rendering; they cried aloud for it; they stammered inexplicably, as though wrestling with it; they groaned, subdued, as though it had overcome them. The meeting opened with the singing of several hymns, which were repeated with increasing vehemence again and again. "Victory, victory, victory all the time," they sang, and one could not but wonder at the extraordinary confidence they seemed to gain from the words. They all remained seated save the stout woman, who stood up with one hand raised aloft and gazed stolidly before her.

But it was the prayers that provoked the most extraordinary manifestations. The people cast themselves down, some kneeling, some lying almost prone, some with their whole bodies stretched prostrate along a seat. A fine-look-

ing man, with a great head of waving hair, began to pray
quietly; but soon he lashed himself into a veritable fury
of petition. His body swayed to and fro, beads of perspira-
tion trickled down his face, and his voice rang out far
beyond the limits of the little hall. The whole audience
was roused. A weird undertone accompanied the ringing
voice—an undertone of sobs, of voices filled with delirious
delight; a crooning, wooing monotone rose and fell and
above it the one voice went on strong and clear.

The people were variously affected. One young man
knelt for a moment with his head buried in his hands
that rested on the bench before him. He gradually raised
himself, suddenly stretched his hands aloft, stared fixedly
at the window through which the afternoon sun streamed,
and parted his lips in a smile. His face took on the rapt
look of one who is gazing into the very heart of an un-
earthly mystery. His lips uttered an endearing incantation
again and again. Another man was smiling through blind-
ing tears, and women were rocking themselves to and fro.
A negro was again and again trying to ejaculate some words
that seemed striving to tear a way out of him, and every
time he ended futilely in a choked-off sob. It was a strange,
chaotic scene, dominated by the one clarion voice that
went on and on like a dominant instrument in an orchestra,
played up to by a whole series of undertones.

When the voice stopped an old spectacled woman dressed
in rusty black, with a careworn face, took up the chain of
petition. Her voice was full of a yearning that arrested attention. It was thin and piping, and pitched in a monotone, but she ran on with a purity of expression that was
the more remarkable because unexpected. Interwoven
with her own words were passages from the choicest Psalms,
and prophecies, making a wonderfully flowing whole. Some

198

people beamed or laughed outright in almost hysterical joy. Some grovelled as though smitten with a sense of utter wretchedness. Men stretched out their hands as if to embrace an unseen presence, or spoke confidingly and intimately as in answer to a heard voice. The negro was choking for utterance, and giving hoarse cries almost amounting to bellowings in the pain of his non-success.

The room was getting unbearably hot. The base of the stove was a glowing red, and over it the air was a-quiver and a-dance, full of flying motes in the slant of a sunbeam. The emotion was becoming unrestrained. When the prayers were done all order was dispensed with. Whoever desired to speak spoke; and at times someone was speaking while someone else was singing. Suddenly a man with a red tie and touseled hair sprang to his feet and said he had a message. The man nominally in charge of the meeting commenced to make some announcement, but after an unintelligible phrase he lapsed into a sudden farrago of nonsense-words and then sat down again. The man with the red tie began to read the lyric words of the Sixty-fifth Psalm. He was no scholar, and his progress was halting. But the assembly's appreciation of the words was remarkable. People took the words up and murmured them, overturning the phrases lovingly on their tongues. Then, without warning, in the midst of the reading a man began with a loud voice to declaim in an unknown tongue. He suddenly collapsed as though the effort had been too much for him, and leaning his hands on the shoulders of another man trailed himself into the vestry. Several other people had messages, including a "sister", who also dropped incomprehensibly at intervals into occult speech, phrases of which she fitted into her language in a most disconcerting manner.

This "gift of tongues" is the most remarkable feature of the meetings. Each person who drops into this mystic speech seems to have a language of his own, as different from that of the others as French from German, or a schoolboy's Latin from either. The first man who gave vent on Saturday seemed to be ringing the changes on a wild "Hallaballoo, hullaballoo"; while from women's lips would trickle a musical rain of incomprehensibility. The set, earnest faces of those who thus gave utterance seemed to suggest, strange though it may seem, that their incantations were meaningful to themselves. While these manifestations were in progress the assembly maintained an awed silence—the only intervals of silence in meetings characterised by chaotic loquacity. It seemed as though these outbursts were regarded as the culminating evidence of the "Power" that had been invoked. Only when they ceased—which sometimes happened with abruptness, sometimes in a trailing murmur—loud cries of praise and joy would be raised. During the evening service the strangest outbursts took place, and it is worthy of note, as an illustration of the import set on these things, that a speaker declared that no other evidence than that of "tongues" was sufficient to show that the Holy Ghost had been given to a man.

The evening meeting was practically a succession of these remarkable breakings forth. The little room was filled practically to its utmost capacity, and to the heat of the stove was added the glare of crude gas jets. The fervour was explosive rather than intense, and after a period of almost violent prayer, during which the larger part of the audience were prostrate, the man whose trumpet voice had led the petitions of the afternoon began to expound the Scriptures.

There followed the most extraordinary scene of the day— a scene than which stagecraft never devised anything more uncannily effective. The speaker had worked himself and his audience to a pitch at which his resonant voice was accompanied by a running fire of fervent ejaculations, when a woman who had been gazing fixedly in front of her began to utter uncouth words. The speaker stopped and the audience fell into silence. Then, in a voice equalling in power that of a man who had been speaking, the woman poured out a wild cataract of seeming nonsense. No sooner had her voice ceased than thin silvery tones, in startling contrast, came from an old man sitting at the front of the hall. "The grass withereth, the flower fadeth, but the word of our God shall stand forever. O Zion, that bringest good tidings, get thee up into the high mountain." And so the fragile voice went piping on through the words of Isaiah.

When the voice had trailed away into silence, a riot of thanksgiving burst out on every hand. The speaker began once more to develop his theme, when the woman's voice, talking the same unknown tongue, again inspired an awed hush. No sooner had she ceased than the silvery tones of the old man, infinitely remote, infinitely gracious, intoned another of the most beautiful passages of Scripture. One was reminded of the visionary old Gaffer Pearce of Masefield's "Nan", fluting his prophecies through the tumult of those about him. So the strange scenes went on, now riotous and ecstatic, now infused with a spirit of abjection or appeal; on the whole confident and self-assertive, but shot here and there with strands of unexpected beauty.

*   *   *

This is as factual and objective an account of the matter as I was capable of writing thirty-one years ago. I have introduced this matter of Evan Roberts and revivalism because of its effect on our select congregation in the Wesleyan chapel. As I have said, only the skirts of that fiery fervour brushed Cardiff ; but merely to feel the backwash of so powerful and enigmatic a wave was to be startled out of the accustomed. All over the country souls were being gathered to God—or so it was believed—and the staid churches and chapels of our city were perhaps a little exercised in conscience that within their own precincts these rushing Pentecostal winds were not creating so much as a draught to stir the curtains. For all the sermons, and all the " special occasions ", and all the class meetings and prayer-meetings and cricket-pitches, when had a soul stood up and declared itself led from darkness into light as in the days when Wesley, like Evan Roberts, had thousands groaning, wailing and gnashing their teeth ?

Anyhow, it was decided that something must be done to get in line with the manifestations that were setting the valleys afire ; and so a few processions were organised through our suburb. There was marching, a pause at street-corners for the singing of hymns and for invitations to attend the chapel services. It was the feeblest of flickers and soon died out. Assuredly, no one in those sedate demonstrations was " possessed ", filled with an over-plus of dynamic life that could fly out and shatter the apathy of the lookers-on. And so it ended as though it had not been, as ineffectual as the Pleasant Sunday Afternoons, for men only, which were organised about this time, and at which, I recall, Mr. Arthur Henderson once addressed us. I do not remember what he had to say.

* * *

Religion, at this time, had a deep hold on me. I had never experienced any such overpowering emotion as was throwing people prostrate throughout Wales; nothing had happened to allow me to speak of myself as " saved " within the meaning of the Plymouth Brethren ; but I did derive a sense of sweetness and exultation from acts of worship. I accepted on the most realistic footing the dogmas of the Church : that Jesus was God and the Son of God ; that he was born of a Virgin ; that, his earthly ministry done, he was crucified, dead, and buried ; that he rose again on the third day, and in the fulness of time ascended into heaven. This was all on the plane not only of the unquestioned but of the unquestionable ; and, about now, I was ripe for the design which, unknown to me, the old Methodist who was my class-leader had been nourishing in his heart. During the summer weeks when he was on holiday I had taken the class for him ; and soon thereafter he startled me with the proposition that I should prepare myself to become a Wesleyan parson. But the poor can't do things in that headstrong fashion. My father had been dead for a long time ; there was a home for a mother and a younger brother and two small sisters to be kept together, and to this task my elder brother and I were addressing ourselves. When my class-leader explained that I should have to go to a training-college at Headingley or Didsbury, and that, though most of my fees would be found, still I might have to provide a fraction of them : well, that put the matter off the footing of the practical for the moment. It had to be left as a dream of something that might be ; and in the meantime I consented to take up the work of a Wesleyan local preacher. In my more depressed moments, I still think of myself as a stickit local preacher.

Memory is vague as to the formalities of that moment. I recall visits to two parsons of the circuit who gave me advice about theological reading, of which during the next few years I did a great deal. There were certain sermons of John Wesley's with which one had to be thoroughly acquainted, and from these I went on to read many other of the founder's sermons. I thought them dull beyond belief, and could not understand how they ever had the effect, which undoubtedly they did have, of throwing great audiences into paroxysms of emotion. I remember, too, being entrusted to the oversight of an old and experienced local preacher and of my trembling apprehension when this man appeared as a member of my first congregation to note and report the way in which I acquitted myself. To me, when it was over, he made no comment except that I should not grasp the lapel of my coat but should seek for a freer method of deportment.

If I forget so much of the happenings of those days, I am not likely to forget the occasion of my first sermon. The sermon itself is gone, utterly and irrecoverably. I cannot recall the text or a word that I uttered. But the occasion is indelible in my mind. The little chapel stood on the high road running through Llandaff. It was nothing but one small oblong room. A boy who had been a school friend of mine, and who later entered an Anglican hostel whence his studies at the University of Wales were directed towards the Church, came with me and sat among the congregation, who numbered six or eight. There was also my supervisor, and with him came his daughter and a young man who was, as they say, paying her attention. This young man accompanied the hymns on a harmonium.

Such was my first congregation, and when it was over my friend and I came out into the summer evening and made our way back to our suburb through the Llandaff fields. The congregation from the Cathedral was streaming out into the warm dusk—so different a congregation from mine!—but I did not permit myself to think that some day perhaps I would speak not to ten people in an oblong room but to a congregation as numerous as this which now was surging through the fields to meet and mingle with the congregation from our own Wesleyan Cathedral coming from the opposite direction. No; I do not think I ever seriously entertained the thought that I might become a parson. Here was this local preaching job into which I had drifted because my inclinations went that way, and I did it as well as I could; but, despite gentle and persistent urgings from my class-leader, my mind never got to grips with the idea of the ministry. Years later, that Wesleyan parson whom I have spoken of as my friend heard me preach, and said : " If you ever took to the ministry, you'd have small but select audiences." I could never be sure whether or not it was a compliment.

Up to the time of my leaving Cardiff to go and work in Bradford at the age of twenty-two, my name remained, as the Wesleyans say, " on the plan ". The " plan " is a periodical sheet, issued by each " circuit " of Methodism, showing who will preach where on any given occasion. A circuit has two or three chapels with a minister attached to each, and two or three small chapels with no minister. As a rule, the local preachers take the services in these smaller chapels, but this is not invariable. Sometimes they are visited by ministers, and sometimes local preachers take the services in the larger chapels. I suppose altogether I did about four years of local preaching, and this was during the busiest time of my life. I was working in our local newspaper office throughout the day as a taker-down of reports telephoned from correspondents throughout South Wales. Then in the evening I was employed upon the reporting staff, and between such engagements as I had to " cover " I was attending all sorts of classes at the Technical School. To fit sermon-making into this sort of life was not easy, and there were times when the notion of going to college at Didsbury or Headingley, and having but the one matter to engage me, became as alluring as the thought of a good week-end in bed. But my brother's death in the midst of all this ended that notion for ever. The main support of a considerable family was now on my shoulders; journalism was ready money; and though I kept up the local preaching as long as I remained in Cardiff, the improvement of myself as a journalist was henceforth my main thought. I wanted to leave the local paper with which I had been connected, in one capacity and another, since I was a child. A reporter was wanted by *The Yorkshire Observer* in Bradford. I applied for the job and got it.

The conclusion of this story of my connection with Wesleyan Methodism can be quickly told. I remained in Bradford for three and a half years. Throughout that time I was a member of a Wesleyan congregation, but my name was no longer " on the plan ". Then, in the early disturbing days of the first World War I moved to Manchester. I did not become a member of any congregation there, and I was not there long. I joined the Army. I returned to Manchester when the war was over, and still I joined no congregation. Nor have I done to this day, whether Wesleyan or any other.

In those post-war Manchester years my home was a stone's-throw from the Didsbury college at which I once dreamed of being a student. I had some slight connection with the place, for one of my army acquaintances was now a student there, and I occasionally visited him in this once fabulous domain. Moreover, my old parson-friend was an examiner who came to Manchester when the periodical examinations were in progress at the college, and he always stayed at my house on those occasions. We spent some good evenings in my study with our pipes going, but I cannot recall that we ever discussed religious matters. My own religious opinions were in a state of chaos. I found that I no longer believed what I had taken to be central and crucial. What I *did* believe was something that never throughout the next twenty years engaged my serious thought. If I had been challenged at any time during those years, I should have disclaimed the description of atheist but frankly have accepted the description of agnostic. These matters, I should have said, are accessible to speculation but not to knowledge. We *cannot* know. One of the most tentative, shy and spineless guesses ever penned would have expressed my state of mind. Tennyson is the author, and I have put into italics the shambling reservations with which he expresses himself :

> Yet still we *trust* that *somehow* good
> *May* be the final end of ill.

I could have ventured no farther than that at any time between the two wars, and what enabled me to go farther was a sudden realisation that the central teaching of Jesus amounted to no more than this : That God is love, and that the affairs of men will never get out of their sorry tangle till they see and acknowledge this and live in the brotherhood which it implies. Of course, I had heard this all my life, but now for the first time I *realised* it.

The times were propitious for re-examination of one's

208

values. Twice within my lifetime the world had been given to the physical waste and chaos of war and to its moral squalor. It would have been easy to take the common view that " it's all the Germans' fault ", and to rest in the happy assurance that once the Germans had been rendered impotent we could take up again the nineteenth-century Liberal dream of steady automatic progress. But I could not do this : I could not believe that this was true. Too much was wrong that had nothing to do with Germany and the Germans. The cheapness and faithlessness of our national life between the wars, the decay of our industries, the hunger of our people, the gross materialism of such ambition as was anywhere to be discerned : all these things were there up to the moment of the war's outbreak, and Germany had nothing to do with them. Whether the war had come or not, a reckoning of some sort would have come ; and as for the war itself, it was this shiftless and unimaginative attitude that delivered us all but naked into the hands of our enemies. The state of mind which had permitted our ships to rot in every creek while Jarrow became a by-word, which cared little or nothing that our coal valleys were peopled with haunted and disillusioned men : this state of mind could have few stones to throw at the wolves across the water if they began to lick their lips on sight of such accessible and defenceless sheep. And I don't mean defenceless in a military sense only.

No ; the war had blown things sky-high ; but many of them were rotting things, and it seemed to me that it was behind and beyond the war, not in it, that we must look for the source of putrescence. One of the damnable things about war is that it takes too many men's minds off this essential research ; and when it is over they are—and this is not to be wondered at—too exhausted for the enterprise.

It chanced that at this time a friend sent me a copy of Jeremy Collier's translation of *The Emperor Marcus Antoninus : his Conversations with Himself*. This was the first edition, published by Richard Sare " at Grays-Inn Gate in Holborn " in 1701 : the first time the famous *Meditations* had been rendered into English. In the disastrous days of 1940, when shock after shock made Europe reel beneath the still young and buoyant strength of the Nazis, I found it difficult to give my mind to the daily work. One morning when I went into my study I picked up this old book and began to read. " The greatest part of your trouble lies in your fancy, and therefore you may disengage yourself when you please. I'll tell you which way you may move more freely and give ease and elbow-room to your mind. Take the whole world into your contemplation, and the little time you are to live in it. Consider how fast the scenes are shifted, and how near the end of all things lies to their beginning ! But then, the extent of Duration in which we are nothing concerned ! The ages before our birth and after our death are both infinite and unmeasurable. Whatever makes a Figure now will quietly decay and disappear ; and those that gaze upon the Ruins of Time will be buried under them."

This was, indeed, stern and Stoic comfort, not the warm pap of to-morrow's Utopia but a cold astringent douche to steady the outlook for to-day. Thereafter, I made a practice of beginning the morning not by sitting down to my desk with a mind inflamed by all the surging incertitude of the times, but by standing up and reading erect for half-an-hour or so from Marcus Aurelius. I found it a salutary and strengthening custom, and towards the end of the morning, instead of working on to the last moment, I would stop to give myself half-an-hour of doing nothing but sitting in my chair, relaxed and meditative.

In this way, I read twice through the *Meditations*, and by then it seemed to me that no day should be begun with a plunge straight into " business ", whatever that business might be. A few moments of quietness in the company of a supreme and tranquil mind seemed to pay dividends that would make a company promotor lick his chops. It is so easy to begin the day with a rush through the morning paper and a rush through the morning mail, and then to make a rush at the work in hand : so easy, but I now think so foolish and so unnecessary. It is like playing the fiddle before it has been keyed up : it will be off pitch all day. " The things that are seen are temporal, but the things that are unseen are eternal." We treat our minds as we are now being urged to treat our landscape. Some American engineers have been over here investigating our coal-mining methods, and a newspaper correspondent, commenting on this, says : " An American engineer close to the official mission disgustedly "—note that, *disgustedly*—" tells me that 3,000,000 added tons could be extracted in the same period were the same ruthless methods, *permanently* defacing the scenery, applied in Britain as are used in the United States." This is a reference to what is called " strip-mining ", peeling off irrecoverably the thin layer of earth on which, ultimately, all life on this planet depends. The world indeed is too much with us, getting and spending ; and one cannot wonder at Wordsworth's vehement denial of all this : " Dear God, I'd rather be a pagan, suckled in a creed outworn." And as with the earth, so with our own beings, we rush hurriedly into getting and spending, and strip off the sensitive apprehensions which, if left to absorb the sun and the rain, would be the medium through which heavenly influences could beget earthly fruits. As it is, too many of us earn the name of realists, practical men, by exposing to life nothing but a hard and igneous carapace.

*   *   *

After the second reading of the *Meditations*, I began the mornings with readings from the Bible, and it was during these readings of a book neglected for a quarter of a century that the central importance of a loving god and love of the brethren took possession of my mind. Of course, as a theory of Christian conduct this had always

212

been known to me, as to everyone in Christendom. But that is another matter. I remember how an old swimming instructor used to say to me in the Manchester baths : "Now I want you to realise that water doesn't suck you down : it holds you up. I know you can't swim, but just take a deep breath and lie on the water. You'll find it holds you up." All very well ! But being of little faith, I didn't trust the water, and even now don't trust it, and so to this day will never venture far from the shore. To know the theory of balance is one thing ; to find suddenly that one is riding the bicycle is another.

How then did I come to *know*, with a final and absolute certainty, that men would never find peace save in the love of God ? Simply by the observation of opposites, simply by a watch upon cause and effect in operation on every hand. No one could pretend that the affairs of the human race were conducted on the basis of love of the brethren. Every amelioration of the lot of the poor came not as a gift of love to what a loving thought demanded, but as something reluctantly squeezed, after acrimonious debate, out of superfluity. One had but to consider the history of the social legislation brought forward by Asquith's government. "If thine enemy hunger, feed him." That was the command of love ; and these were not our enemies ; which is perhaps why the command was not held to apply. It was the same, in its general outline, wherever one looked at the relationships of men. Trades and industries were not conducted with a view to the benefit of those who worked in them, but primarily as means of earning dividends on investments. Combines and cartels seized upon the necessaries of life, not, one can be sure, because love of mankind had put into the monopolists' hearts the thought of providing service at the most reasonable price. Internationally, there was small sign, if any, of thought for the creation of preservation of harmonious living. The balancing of national budgets was the chief aim of national enterprise, and so a superabundance of national thought was absorbed by " getting and spending ". One small instance of this sort of thing is that our relationships with certain countries in the Middle East are said to have " deteriorated " because we preferred to buy our tobacco elsewhere. A struggle for " markets " in a world increasingly made up of countries which wanted to manufacture for themselves rather than buy from others, and an increasing tendency to make things not because they were necessary to anyone on earth but because through them commerce hoped to " create " new markets : all this, backed by an enormous apparatus for " boosting " these unnecessary things, was the matter of the world's main preoccupation.

No one could pretend that this welter of competing commercial states was a world of love, or that the methods by which the newly-arisen " ideologies " sought to promulgate themselves were the methods of love. The air of the world, long before the explosion came, was charged with menace, and men walked with a fixed and fascinated stare upon the

thorns they were piling before their own breasts. Since
what we are and do to-day are a necessary outcome of what
we were and did in the days that are gone, war is the outcome of the general condition of human living in the years
we are considering. *Ex nihilo nihil.* There can be no tree
without a seed.

It would be putting the matter too forcibly to say that
we were living in a world of hate. We were living rather
in a world of fear ; and fear, not hate, is the antithesis of
love. "Perfect love casteth out fear"—not hate. Fear is
a more dangerous and poisonous condition than hate,
which can take on the large proportions of grandeur ;
while fear (save the "fear of God", when that is rightly
understood) is a condition that diminishes and never en-
larges those upon whom it preys. Fear is a privy vice, to
be recognised rarely for itself but mainly by its public face,
which is greed. The man who fears life will be for ever
snatching at this and that in his endeavour to build up
defences against it ; but the man who loves life will cast
himself upon its bosom, knowing the companionship that
"doth the raven feed, and providently caters for the
sparrow".

It is strange to observe how, in time of war, we see the
necessity of doing what we will not do in times of peace.
We lay upon ourselves the obligations of feeding and
clothing the needy and caring for the sick. And are not
these Christian virtues ? Not necessarily. Why are we
expending our substance upon such things ? Is it for

love of these people ? Or because of our fear that chaos
and pestilence, like the Red Death in Poe's tale, may
spread from them to us ? To take another instance.
Major Yeats-Brown, in his book, *Martial India*, tells how
the newly-enlisted troops in India were used in an organisation that fought against the recent famine. Young
officers and N.C.O.s, he points out, gained valuable experience of command, and problems of supply, so vital to
warfare, were studied in practice.

For myself, I believe that the virtue of an action—that
is, its final effectiveness—springs directly from the motive
behind it, and this was something upon which St. Paul
insisted in one of the most striking passages he ever wrote.
If I speak with the tongues of men and angels, he says, if
I have the gift of prophecy and all knowledge, if I give
all my goods to feed the poor, if I go so far as to sacrifice
life itself, giving my body to be burned, all this will have
no real and final effect—" it profiteth me nothing "—if I
have not love. Not what you do, but why you do it, constitutes the point of virtue; and the mind is fascinated by
the prospect opened up as one considers what the consequences might have been if the rich nations of the world
had borne the blessings of food and care to the poor and
needy outside their own borders not as a by-product and
sanitary precaution of war but from simple love of mankind.

But, as one considered the world between the wars, one
saw that such things were not happening, that naked fear

and greed were the main determinants of action, and that
these were producing a world of disharmony. Now as it
is impossible to conceive of anyone being astray unless one
has first conceived the idea of the road that he should be
following, and as it is impossible to think of an instrument
being off-pitch unless the true note is present to the mind :
so it is impossible to speak of this world being in disharmony
unless one admits the conception of harmony. The night
may be dark, and we far from home, but there is a home,
and we know it. We admit, in short, that harmony is the
true condition of life, the true substance of the world's
being, and that our sense of lostness, of being in the dark,
springs from nothing but our having lost touch with this
vital principle. Those who have been fortunate enough
to know earthly love know that love and harmony are two
names for one thing. Since, then, we admit that harmony
is the principle of the universe, we admit that love is the
principle of the universe, and thus we are able to accept the
teachings of Jesus that God is love.

*　　　　*　　　　*

Thus simply—too simply, perhaps, for any theologian !
—I came upon the re-discovery, or more truly the discovery, of God. There was nothing dramatic about this,
no sense of a soul being saved ; and the more I think of
souls and salvation the more I distrust the drama of " con-
version ". Souls, like brains and bodies, are apt to mature,

217

if at all, slowly, steadily, by the simple procedure of discovering their right sustenance and keeping to it. No; there was nothing but a calm assurance that these few things are true : that as disaster follows upon disharmony in the world, one may assume that the world's principle is harmony; that love and harmony are one; that Jesus was therefore teaching the central truth of life when he told us that the principle of the universe is love. Since no principle can be violated without chaos, it follows that men will never know peace, love, harmony, till the love of God the father is worked out here on earth in the shape of love of the brethren.

*   *   *

I said a good way back that I should have to define my terms, to say what I meant when I used such words as God and the spiritual life. The time to do this seems now to have come. What do I mean when I speak of God the father ?

The Anglican, repeating his creed, says : " I believe in God the Father almighty, maker of Heaven and Earth," and to go no farther than that, we are brought up with a jerk. For when this Creed was written, neither Heaven nor earth meant what it means now. Heaven, to the common mind of that time, was a country above the sky where God sat upon a throne, with his Son, who was also himself, sitting at his right hand, with a hierarchy of heavenly beings surrounding him, and with the host of the redeemed growing daily as soul after soul arrived, the toils of this earth done. Such was the Heaven of which God was the Maker ; and as for the earth, it was this sphere upon which we live, this pleasant place of sea and land, wood and plain, mountain and valley, peopled by man and the birds, beasts and fishes, all existing as they came from God's hand in consequence of a week's work not so long ago. There might be some dispute as to the date, some argument as to a thousand years this way or that. An ancient copy of Hadyn's *Dictionary of Dates* which I possess, dated 1860, which was a year after the publication of Darwin's *Origin of Species*, has this note on the age of the earth : " There are about 140 different dates assigned to the Creation. Some place it 3,616 years before the birth of our Saviour ; the epoch is fixed by the Samaritan Pentateuch at 4700 B.C. ; the Septuagint makes it 5872 ; the authors of the Talmud make it 5344 ; and different chronologers, to the number of 120, make it vary from the Septuagint date to 3268. Dr. Hales fixes it at 5,411."

This, then, was the general notion : that roughly five thousand or six thousand years before Jesus was born God had fashioned the earth and furnished it. The cosmos was something that few minds endeavoured to apprehend. The whirling ball of earth, seething, steaming and contracting, boiling and freezing, throughout thousands of millions of years ; the creeping and flying and swimming creatures, changing, modifying, adapting ; the uncountable

219

multitude of the stars that died in the day and flawed like tracer bullets to show God's handiwork upon the depths of night; the frozen wastes between these glittering balls, and the unplumbed space beyond them containing unapprehendable mysteries: all this was something different from the conception of a seven-day conjuror producing the ready-made bag of tricks. And now, when we say that we believe in the "Maker of Earth" this is the Maker: this plodder whose infinite patience proceeds from amoeba to man across an experimental span whose duration the mind faints to contemplate. And, to take it farther back, there was the perhaps even more remarkable procedure from nothing to the amoeba.

The jibe that Christians were wont to think of their God as an old gentleman with a long beard, alternately chiding and praising: a sort of Father Christmas who rewarded the good children but drove implacably past the chimney-pots of the naughty: this jibe is ill-tempered and unimaginative. The old belief was founded on a deep-rooted tendency—even need—of the human heart to comfort itself amid the immensities and perplexities of this mortal life. To feel the need to turn to a Father, and to be accompanied into his presence by a Son, is not to confess a weakness but to accept a fact that seems to lie at the root of our being: and there is wisdom in accepting facts. That the Roman Catholics have added a loving woman to the potent intercessors for God's grace is nothing that can cause surprise to an imaginative mind.

But when we have said and done with all this, there remains the truth that these are but our human fumblings to formulate what, in fact, can never be formulated, and we are reduced to Zophar's cry : " Canst thou by searching find out God ? Canst thou find out the Almighty unto perfection ? " But such a cry is not without hope, for to admit that a quest cannot succeed " to perfection " is of itself to admit that it is not a wild-goose chase, that at any rate there are certain elements of the matter which we can hold on to.

We begin, then, our quest for " God the Father almighty, the Maker ", by reminding ourselves that, by every fact of experience and logic, nothing, literally nothing, can come into existence without a prior cause. *Ex nihilo nihil.* Of the nature and purpose of this vast, awe-inspiring and complicated process at which we have given no more than a fleeting glimpse : this process extending backwards into unimaginable abysses of time and using for its materials on the one hand the fragile mayfly that dances in the sunshine for an hour and is gone, and on the other flaming worlds writhing their skins into mountains and scooping out the hollows in which the oceans roar ; this process which sends stars headlong through the firmament like handfuls of scattered pebbles, and which, so far as our frail imaginations can grasp, will go on to a time beyond the farthest reach of thought : of the nature and purpose of all this we can know nothing *by reason*. But of its *reality*, we can be in no doubt, and since it exists, it must have a cause, a Maker.

Now that this Maker is what theology calls a " personal "

God is not something which I can accept within any meaning that my mind can apply to the word " person ", and yet
to speak merely of a " principle " fails to express what I feel
in the matter. It is true that, in this business of living, success or failure, within the real meaning of those words,
depends upon the degree to which our lives are gladly sur-
rendered to the guidance of those principles which lie behind all that we understand by value. But what lies
behind principle itself ? For the intangible, as of the tangible, it must be true that nothing comes from nothing.
Therefore behind the principle lives something of whose
reality the principle is the shadow ; and in that word *lives* is
the essence of my belief in God. I cannot say that I believe in a personal God, for our human conception of personality has dwarfed the word to belittling proportions. I
can say that I believe in a living God : " One God, who
ever lives and moves." And here I do not take refuge in
the old paradox *Credo quia incredibile*. Rather I say : " I
believe this because any other belief is incredible." To
believe in Nothing as the cause of the supernal processes
by which the cosmos, and man in it, have come into being :
this is indeed the supreme renunciation of reason. Yet
men who will tell you that to find two rows of bricks piled
one upon another is evidence that a mind and a hand have
been at work will tell you also that the building up of
fiery worlds and their launching into space is no evidence
for a living cause. Not that the mind's consent is all that
is here in question. For the mind might well consent to

the idea of a living God and yet see in Him a cynical maniac to whom the only fitting words we might speak would be those of the *Rubáiyát*:

> For all the Sin wherewith the Face of Man
> Is blackened, Man's Forgiveness give—and take!

Evil and pain—the mental and physical manifestations of one notion—have been the stumbling-blocks of many; and the objections they raise are not lightly to be put aside. Is it possible to believe in a loving God as well as in a living God? There is no need to do more than keep one's eyes open for the space of a single day to see the deep interfusion of pain in the life of the world. The mouse trembling before the cat; the gold-crests ravaged by the jays; the fly in the web; the ant's universe crushed by a careless foot: these are minute illustrations of what seems to be an immense principle. One half of the world lives by killing and eating the other half, and this, on the surface, seems so revolting that the vegetarian turns in disgust from the whole business. But the vegetarian alternative, if adopted by us all, would modify the human way of living in a revolutionary fashion. If sheep and cattle were not bred for food, which means if they were not continuously killed off, then their unhindered breeding would fill our countryside with flocks and herds that would make inconceivable inroads upon the food the vegetarian demands. Rabbits, increasing by millions annually, to say nothing of

223

pigs and goats, would eat us up like a plague of locusts, and such fields as we managed to bring to harvest would be stripped by the partridges and pheasants that had been allowed to multiply in the woods. It is easy to see that the time would speedily come when vegetarian man in crowded countries like those of Europe would realise that, in a competition between himself and vegetarian animals for the means of livelihood, the animals were winning. He would then have either to introduce wolves and jackals to help maintain the balance between animal and human life—though these would soon prove to be as intractable as Hengist and Horsa—or kill the surplus beasts himself. Since his original objection is to living by killing, his dilemma would be acute, for, whether or not he ate what he killed, it is clear that, in the not very long run, he would have to kill to live. His only alternative, then, would be frankly to accept the competition of the animals and to make what he could of life on the planet in those conditions. One does not have to think far to see that it would be life in startlingly different conditions from any that we now enjoy. Husbandry as we know it would be impossible, and industry without husbandry as its basis would be impossible too. That industry has forgotten for the moment that husbandry is its basis is beside the point. It would soon learn. Napoleon at any rate understood it when he said that an army marches on its stomach. Vulcan cannot go far without Ceres.

This brief and, I fear, insufficient outline of some objections to the vegetarian position is not put down here merely in the hope of discrediting that position. It is put down as part of any attempt to understand the incidence of pain and death in the world. Terror, pain, and death appear to be inextricably mixed up with living itself; and when you go below the surface of simple and uncomplicated killing for food, you find what appear to be most complicated and ingenious methods of bringing life into being through processes of torture. That the germs of one creature's life should be deposited in the vital organs of another and come to fullness only by the slow and one must presume painful destruction of the host : this and such other manifestations of life depending on the annihilation of life pull up the mind upon the brink of a fearful chasm. Pain engendered by the sadism of man, so woefully increasing in the contemporary world, is one thing and might be dismissed from the question as a necessary ingredient of a great good, freewill; but pain springing from the roots of life itself, seeming to be one of the bases on which life is planted, having nothing to do with the free will of man or any other creature, but handed out willy-nilly, apparently with no discrimination, so that we see many of the loveliest and the best enduring years of torture : this is another thing, and one not to be disregarded.

A small strange point occurs to my mind, and it is this. The orthodox Christian, who accepts Jesus as very God of very God, likes to insist that *in all things* he suffered as we do and knew every pang of human flesh. But, so far as the record goes, there is no evidence that he experienced human illness and the pain consequent thereupon. The record is of abundant and indefatigable bodily fitness. The final pains of death in a violent and brutal form, yes. The " ills that flesh is heir to ", no, so far as we are told. I do not know that this has any significance : I put it down simply as a point that comes to me.

For myself, I shall not try either to explain or to explain away the problem of pain. I have read books that endeavour to do so, books that would even make of pain a beneficent angel. They leave me unconvinced, if only because pain so often strikes at creatures organically developed to a pitch at which the pangs must be excruciatingly felt, yet incapable of drawing any of those moral and spiritual benefits which some expositors tell us reside in pain rightly borne. Even if it could be shown that human pain has spiritual significance, this would not answer our questions about pain that can have no significance. Mr. Richard Perry's book *I went a-Shepherding*, telling of his experiences among Highland flocks, has some nauseating matter. The depredations of what he calls " that terrible and revolting pest " the blow-fly sicken the imagination. The afflicted creatures are literally eaten alive, till they are nothing but hollow things with nothing left but the precarious strength to stand on their legs. " A mist would often come before my eyes ", Mr. Perry writes, " when I bent to stroke the velvety muzzle and the grizzled toppin curling between the horns of a struck ewe."

226

> New every morning is the love
> Our wakening and uprising prove

Keble sings ; but the morning sun that touches our comfortable pillows falls, too, into the sad grey eyes of the ewes gnawed hollow, shuddering beside a rock. What does *their* wakening prove ?

What then are we to believe ? Accepting as irrefutable a living God, can we claim also to know a loving God ? Nowhere has the matter been explored more profoundly and beautifully than in the great poem that we call *The Book of Job*, and the answer is simply acceptance in the face of all that may be said on the other side. " Let come on me what will. . . . Though he slay me, yet will I wait for him." It is only after this acceptance that Job is able to declare : " I had heard of thee by the hearing of the ear ; but now mine eye seeth thee." And what does the eye see ? This above all : that whatever may be the purpose of pain and evil in the world, the *operative* force is love. All else, finally, is negative. Love is positive. I do not mean that evil is sterile. It begets lavishly in its own kind, but its fruits are death. The fruits of love are life more abundant.

This, I say, is to be seen by the eye ; and it is to be seen on every hand. As I have already pointed out, it is to be seen to-day most clearly by the observation of its opposite. If fear, greed, hate produce, as we see them producing, the destruction of life and of the loveliest works of man's heart and hand and mind ; if they ingeminate, as

227

they are ingeminating, not hope for the future but the thorns on which to-morrow we shall breed, then it is a plain deduction that love which gives and not demands, which seeks to serve and not to dominate, which " vaunteth not itself " rather than puts forward " those claims which a great power is entitled to advance " : this love may be expected to achieve the converse of what so darkly besets our present and broods like a devil unexorcised upon our future.

This we may deduce by a consideration of opposites ; but the plain and positive validity of love is, too, a matter for the observation of any uncalloused heart. We *know* that harmony, which is the ultimate consequence of love, is achieved not indeed by the annihilation of personality —let that be as full-flowered as it may—but by its refusal to insist and overbear, by its adjustment to the needs of other personalities, by the service of each by the other. There are circumstances in which love may call for sacrifice, but sacrifice is not necessarily a part of the love-harmony. The full development of all that the fiddles can give is enhanced and not diminished by the groundwork of the drums doing what they are called upon to do. The harmony is destroyed only when the one becomes so overbearing as to throw the other out of concert. Love is not, as it is sometimes said to be, give and take. That is a lesser matter : that is expediency. Love is unfettered giving : the throwing of one's fullest and truest note, regardless of the cost to oneself, into the universal harmony.

We know in our hearts that this is how we *desire* to live.

228

We know, too, that when in some small measure and for some little time we thus have lived we experience the ineffable and unmistakable Yea, the sense that this life of love has unquestionable sanctions. And this, for me, is the Yes to the question whether the living God is a loving God. It is the life of love that we feel fully at one with him, with the mysterious intimations that flow into the heart in moments of reverie and give us peace. It is then, accepting all those elements that seem, in isolation, to be discordant, that we say : " I will trust, and will not be afraid."

* * *

The Apostles' Creed goes on : " And in Jesus Christ his only Son our Lord, who was conceived by the Holy Ghost, born of the Virgin Mary."

The narratives of St. Mark and St. John say nothing of the circumstances surrounding the birth of Jesus : they begin with the opening of his public ministry. Matthew says of Mary : " She was found with child of the Holy Ghost " ; and Luke causes the angel Gabriel to appear to her and announce : " Thou shalt conceive." In both these narratives, then, the Holy Ghost is the begetter and Mary conceives. Who the begetter is according to the Apostles' Creed does not appear. It was the Holy Ghost, the Creed tells us, who "conceived" the child and Mary who bore him without, apparently, even having conceived him. Presumably, the Creed writers meant (if they were following the record) begotten by the Holy Ghost, conceived by the Virgin Mary. As it is, it is a jumbled and meaningless sentence, unless we are to explain the word "by", in the phrase "conceived by the Holy Ghost", as meaning "conceived by the interposition or agency of the Holy Ghost". So long as the Church adheres to the doctrine of the Virgin birth, it should clarify this sentence.

For me, it does not matter. The whole story has the charm and appealing interest of a folk-tale. The Bible is full of comparable matter. There are still those who believe that God created the world in seven days, that a serpent held conversations with Eve, and that Jacob literally wrestled throughout a long night with an angel. The spiritual content of poetry is not diminished because the mould into which it is cast is clearly of the imagination. Shelley is not discredited because we do not believe that Prometheus was literally chained to a rock with a vulture eating his liver, or Homer because the sirens could not produce identity cards. Freeman says : "A false anecdote may be good history"; and "falsity", in any case, is not the word one would care to apply to folk-beliefs. That these may be spread as wide as the world itself and yet have no rational basis appears from a study of witchcraft, with its conclusion that the undoubted power of witches was based not in what they were but in what they were believed to be, even in what some of them sincerely believed themselves to be. Once the belief was withdrawn, the power went, too.

230

But the power of beauty and spiritual suggestion that resides in spiritual folk-lore remains incomparable, and only a half-wit would see in it matter of derision. There is the lovely story of the peasant who, in fairly recent times, said that on the eve of the Nativity he had seen the beasts kneeling in their stalls, with tears running down their faces. If there are those who find this a matter for mirth or contempt, we can only dismiss them in sorrow to the steel and concrete fastnesses of their factual existence. To make life more difficult for them (when, with such mental equipment, it must be difficult enough) is another matter. I remember being in the Yorkshire town of Keighley one day in my early twenties and finding there a knot of people surrounding a speaker in an open place. He was a cadaverous person, wearing a battered silk hat, calling himself Dr. Nikola, and he made a habit of going from town to town belittling the Bible by reciting a garbled version of its folk-lore. "So there Mrs. Eve was on that nice summer day in the garden, and along comes Mr. Serpent. He raises his hat"—and here Dr. Nikola illustrated by raising his own hat and bending elegantly from the waist—" and, says he, ' Good afternoon, Mrs. Eve. Would you like a bite of my apple ? ' "

That was the satirical level of Dr. Nikola, and, of course, he got his horse-laughs from a handful of village louts and hobbledehoys. He was arrested soon after under the Blasphemy Acts and sent to prison, and it is difficult to know whom to pity the more : this trivial half-wit or those who believed religion so paltry and thin-skinned a Sebastian that it would wince from his blotting-paper darts. Those were the days when the long Liberal government that preceded the last war was giving to the country the greatest social ameliorations that any one government has ever enacted in Great Britain. And with what howls they were received! One would have imagined that to make the lot of the poor a little easier was the devil's own work. Dowagers competed for the honour of being fined for refusing to stick stamps on servants' insurance cards. No one invoked the Blasphemy Acts against them; but if the holy spirit is that which unites men in love and mercy, then I am aware of no acts under which they might more suitably have been proceeded against.

*   *   *

In this examination of the religious influences that have been encountered in the course of my life, this strikes me as significant : neither among the Plymouth Brethren, nor among the Wesleyans, nor in the course of the hundreds of sermons and discussions I have listened to as a newspaper reporter—Convocations of York, Wesleyan conferences, and many other such assemblages—I have never once heard the Virgin birth of Jesus or his bodily resurrection from the dead examined and explained. Spoken of, yes ; but that is another matter. But always spoken of as something about which there could be no doubt, something that was taken for granted. I once asked a parson why he believed that Jesus was literally God walking upon the earth, and the only answer he could give—an inconclusive and unjustifiable one it seemed to me—was that he was either that or the biggest humbug that ever lived.

The notion of God appearing among men is not exclusively Christian. Krishna, for example, is represented in the Bhagavad-gita as saying : " Unborn, of imperishable soul, the Lord of all creatures, taking upon me my own nature, I arise by my own power. For whenever, O Son of Bharata, there is decay of righteousness, then I create myself, for the protecting of the good and for the destroying of evildoers, and for the establishing of righteousness I arise from age to age."

This is a point that cuts both ways, as G. K. Chesterton was quick to point out in a controversy with Robert Blatchford. If, said Chesterton (I am roughly paraphrasing his words), the idea of the incarnation had occurred to only a few people, then one might more reasonably doubt it than if it had occurred to many people in many times. The almost universal belief in it, in one form or another, is surely, he said, an argument for it, not against it. But Chesterton here landed himself in a difficulty, for the orthodox point of view, which was the one he ultimately defended, could not, whatever he might say, accept the position which Blatchford pointed out. It could not accept the interposition of God into the life of the world at many points. It insisted upon a unique and once-for-all sufficient interposition in the person of Jesus. All human history had been a leading-up to this event; all Messianic hope and prophecy here found fulfilment, and the cry of Jesus upon the cross, "It is finished," was literally a statement of the position. God's plan for the world's redemption was there finished. As indeed it was, insofar as the life and death of Jesus demonstrated that love and sacrifice alone can bridge the gulf between God and man, that these alone can bring to harmony the discords that torture the world. But though, there, that truth received its most awful and re-sounding demonstration, it had been demonstrated many times before, it has been demonstrated many times since; and for the world's salvation it is necessary that it be demonstrated perpetually. Jesus himself seems to rec-ognise this in his saying : "I came to cast fire upon the earth ; and what will I if it is already kindled ? " The universal belief in the incarnation of God seems to me to be nothing but a recognition, for which God be praised, of the divine potentiality of man, a belief that this earthen lamp can burn with the divine fire, not that the Word was once made flesh but that it can become flesh in genera-tion after generation. The life and ministry of Jesus can be encrusted by orthodoxy as thick as it likes with miracle, with Virgin birth and bodily resurrection, but this has not in two thousand years brought us far. We are now so deeply involved in the consequence of our own sin and iniquity that one wonders whether what the world needs is not a voice bidding us to perplex ourselves no more with

234

matters that cannot be proved, and to concern ourselves with the indubitable fact that God who filled the life of Jesus with saving power can so fill every life to whatever its potentiality may be. And this is not something to be wrested with agony from God. The love of God is not a boon jealously withheld. "Fear not, little flock; for it is your Father's *good pleasure* to give you the kingdom."

One thing about this kingdom is that you must take it or leave it. Within it, the rule holds absolutely that you cannot serve God and Mammon. If it were decided, for example, that those inventions of the devil called "V-weapons" should be for ever abandoned, that would be a service of God if the motive behind the abandonment were love of mankind. I have pointed out before, and I believe it to be true, that the validity of action is in motive; and if our motive in suggesting the "outlawing" of V-weapons is simply to save our own skins, knowing as we do that the development of these weapons will soon make the destruction of English towns a mere matter of mathematics, then our motive will not be strong enough to achieve what we desire. If the motive is love of mankind, then not V-weapons alone but all destructive weapons—war itself—will be renounced.

The state of moral shilly-shally in which we find ourselves is perfectly illustrated in one of yesterday's newspapers. A headline flowing across a whole page says: "M.P.s Want All-V-Weapons Outlawed". The paragraph begins: "Many M.P.s want V-bombs outlawed and international commissions, with extensive powers, established to see that never again will they threaten the world. They foresee terrible possibilities in the development of the flying-bomb and rocket projectile. Among members of the House of Lords, Lord Brabazon of Tara, expert in air affairs, told me : 'We have only seen the beginning of the V-weapons. Within the next fifteen years, projectiles ten times the weight of V2, their explosive content far deadlier than anything now known, will pin-point cities, fleets at sea, and factories at ranges of several hundred miles. Like the rocket, explosives are also in their infancy. An international body could— and must—make certain that no V-weapon is built anywhere.' "

I am at a loss to understand his lordship's point of view —or rather, I understand it all too well. It is his logic that perplexes me. His point of view is that *we* are in a great danger that will make our fortunate island situation no longer of any avail. Where his logic fails is here : the object of warlike action is precisely to do the things he says will be done : destroy towns, fleets and factories. Because this will be done from a distance, to our intense personal discomfiture, will make no whit of moral difference to the doing of it. What cause has he then to complain ? The words that litter the headlines in every newspaper I take up are " plaster ", " pound ", " pin-point ", and so on. In a word, we are already doing what he fears will be done. Surely, in a world of modern efficiency, no one is going to complain simply because a job is done more quickly and effectively.

To emphasise the logical and moral quagmire in which these objectors to V-weapons find themselves, the next paragraph in this same newspaper is headed "Fleet Air Arm Grows". It begins : "Britain's Fleet Air Arm will be stronger than ever when the war ends. And the Navy wants to keep it so." Does Lord Brabazon of Tara object ? If not, why not ? For the object of an air-arm is the same as the object of a V-weapon : to destroy the material of an enemy and to kill his people.

The day after the interview with Lord Brabazon, there appeared in the newspapers an account of an attack on the Germans in the Gironde estuary. It was headed "Lake of Flame from Liquid Fire Bombs. 460,000 Gallons Drench Gironde Pocket". The report said that this was the first time this new weapon had been used in Europe. "Detonators explode each tank on impact, splashing the flaming contents over an individual area of approximately 60 square yards."

Does Lord Brabazon of Tara object ? No ; because this is *our* weapon. But you may be sure that it will not be only ours for long. Once these chickens are sent abroad, they soon return to roost.

And so I say the Kingdom of God, the kingdom of love and peace, is something you must take or leave. You can't keep the Barracuda and Firefly bombs and the liquid-fire bombs and ask someone else not to keep V-bombs. Bombs are bombs, whencesoever and by whomsoever directed. M.P.s who demand that "all V-weapons be Outlawed" may save their breath. The Kingdom is one and indivisible, and there is no place in it for bombs of any sort.

We are in the dilemma which I have pointed out before : that we are objecting not to war but to the way in which war goes about its business, while all our lives long we do nothing to create the world in which war cannot exist. What are these M.P.s doing to bring nearer the world of love, which is the only alternative to the world of fear with all the bestial panoply that fear provides ? The mere *ad hoc* objection to this phase of war and that is of all futility the most pathetic. There has been in my district an outcry against a proposal to use Bodmin Moor as a bombing school. But our outcry must be not against the siting of bombing-schools but against every manifestation of the spirit that makes them inevitable. So long as our affairs are settled with bombs we shall need bombing-schools. Otherwise, those who, you may be sure, will object on some ground or another to every site proposed, will be among the first to protest, when the next war comes, that we are "unprepared". St. Paul saw, with a spiritual eyesight that we must ourselves acquire, that our fight, to be successful, must not be directed against these trivial physical accidents—the mere flesh and blood of evil—but against its hidden roots. "For our wrestling is not against flesh and blood, but against the principalities, against the powers, against the world-rulers of this darkness, against

the spiritual hosts of wickedness in the heavenly places."
When love is our law, war will not have to be "outlawed"
by any act or parlimentary decision. It will be outlawed
automatically and of necessity, for it cannot then exist
within our law. And that is the only way. You cannot
"outlaw" what is within the scope of the laws by which
you agree to live.

*　　　*　　　*

These are interpretations of the plain teaching of Jesus.
Our salvation lies in seeing and doing these things, in
accepting and working out the spiritual core of the message, rather than in disputation as to Virgin birth or bodily
resurrection : in religion, not in theology. The difference
between a point of religion and a point of theology is that
the one leaps to the acceptance of heart and mind and
admits of no dispute, while the other wrangles its way
noisily through the centuries, and it is usually for points
of theology, not of religion, that people are burned at the
stake and stretched on the rack. The virginity of Mary
is a case in point. The Gospel writers assert that she was
a virgin when Jesus was born, but they do not hesitate
to accept the notion that she ceased to be a virgin and bore
other children to Joseph. Then there arose those who
disputed this and alleged that the other children were not
of Mary ; and Jerome widened the range of the argument
by saying that they were neither of Mary nor of Joseph.

239

He insisted on a perpetually virgin Joseph as well as a perpetually virgin Mary.

It was not until the middle of the fifth century that the
Church, at the Council of Chalcedon, accepted the doctrine of Mary's perpetual virginity. And then there arose
a further question : was she not only a virgin but im-
maculately conceived ? It was long the contention of
the Catholic Church that Mary committed no sin herself,
but, seeing that all are "born in sin", bearing upon their
heads the ancestral curse, how did she stand in relation
to that ? For centuries this was a matter of dispute, and
it was not until 1854, that is within the memory of people
now living, that the Church reached its decision on the
matter. The Immaculate Conception became a dogma of
the Church defined by Pius IX in these words : "The
doctrine which holds that the Blessed Virgin Mary, from
the first instant of her conception, was, by a most singular
grace and privilege of Almighty God, in view of the merits
of Jesus Christ, the redeemer of the human race, preserved
from all stain of Original Sin, is a doctrine revealed by
God, and therefore to be firmly and steadfastly believed by
all the faithful."

Mankind succeeded for the better part of two thousand
years to get along without having this point settled, as it
can always get along without having theological points
settled, but it cannot get along without deciding what its
attitude is to be to the matter of religion. Points of theology can be decided for us by the Churches : I for one

am very willing to leave it to them : but the matter of
religion, the acceptance or rejection of the belief in a loving
God and of the duty of a loving life : this is something
each must settle for himself.

If it be claimed that the "miraculous" elements in
the life of Jesus are the sanction by which he is entitled
to claim our allegiance ; that, if we reject these, we reject
the touch of God, the signature by which the authenticity
of the masterpiece is recognized, then we reply that not for
a moment do we accept the validity of such an argument,
antique and time-honoured though it may be. We ask
no other sanction for the life of love than the knowledge
that it achieves what is promised for it. It gives peace. It
casts out fear. It induces in the soul that has experienced
it the certitude of harmony with the purposes of life, the
certitude that only the achievement of that harmony can
give, either to the individual or to the race, the exquisite
humour that makes man's brawling assertiveness too mean
and shabby a thing to be attractive any longer. We become men and put away childish things.

This, I say, can be known, and abundantly has been
known, as the inevitable and infallible consequence of the
life of love ; and in that infallibility is the sanction. Only
the eternally fixed is infallible ; and I know of nothing else,
amid all the vicissitudes of human life, that *is* fixed save
this. There is no promise that we shall not labour, only
that we shall be able to carry the burden ; there is no promise that we shall not suffer, only that suffering may be

241

overcome if by nothing else than the brevity and transience of human life itself; no promise that we shall not sin and falter and fall, only that love can redeem the sin, and strengthen the faltering and pick up the fallen. Nothing else can do it, but that love can do it, has done it, and will do it, is the supreme fact of human existence. It is the only panacea. Only within its bounds shall we find the Four Freedoms and any other freedoms there may be.

*   *   *

This is my faith; this is as far as I have been able to advance towards the knowledge and love of God. I believe that, before the birth of Jesus, God was manifesting Himself to the world in lives bearing testimony to this belief, and that He is continuously doing so. Many of these lives have been lived, since the birth of Jesus, by people who never heard his name. That Jesus was divinely appointed as the only Mediator between God and man and that there can be no salvation save through him leaves in a sorry case the teeming generations of the pre-Christian world and the countless millions to-day born outside the boundaries of Christendom. No : the touchstone must be the life of love, and that affords more rather than less reason why, coming into the presence of God, we who take Jesus as our Master, should come in his name, for in him we have fully been shown how the Word, which is love, can become flesh, which is man. And this is the

242

Incarnation by which God perpetually renews Himself in the world.

*   *   *

" I believe in the resurrection of the body and the life everlasting."

It is a strange thing that the Churches which distrust the flesh so deeply that they have evolved the doctrines of the Immaculate Conception and the Virgin birth so that no grossness of this sinful envelope should attach to the person of Jesus, hold to the doctrine that this vile body shall rise. Yet in truth most of us have had enough of the body when the time comes to leave it. " Gladly I lived and gladly die, and I lay me down with a will." " My little body is a-weary of this great world." And in the immense traditional lore of spectres and apparitions the body has no place. There is form without substance, a chill adumbration of fog and mist : nothing of the warmth of our body's rosy contours. The blood is drained away ; the wavering simulacrum is sustained by nothing that a cock's crow cannot dissipate or the first light of morning crumble. To recall our dead even in this fashion as the pitiful exhalation of a fen, dubiously and for but a moment accorded some attributes that permit recognition : even this is a testimony rather of our yearning for the departed than of their concern to revisit the glimpses of the moon. There is, indeed, little in the deep heart of humanity that really believes in the resurrection of the body, though the new smart of bereavement, uncalloused by the passage of years, clings to the hope of reunion in the form that was dear and familiar within " the warm precincts of the cheerful day ". Then, indeed, when the grave has newly closed upon some once lovely head or the fire has consumed it, we may feel a passion of longing for a morning in which, as Newman puts it,

> those angel faces smile,
> Which I have loved long since and lost awhile.

For myself, here I stand upon the brink of the unknown, utter and unplumbed. I have never seen so much as a ghost nor met anyone whose adventures in that direction have satisfied me of validity. All I can say of a surety is that I believe in the perpetual existence of the spiritual life. If we accept, as we must, the theory of the indestructibility of matter, no less must we accept the indestructibility of the spirit with which matter is informed. Having known something of the brightness with which that spirit may burn within its corporal envelope, I cannot believe that it is lost and utterly cast away. But in what form it persists, and whether by any reach of the imagination its continuance could be known as " personal ", it is not within my competence to understand. That the will of God here on this earth achieves itself through the instrumentality of persons is a self-evident fact, but by what means that will is done beyond the grave is hidden from us. It may involve the utter annihilation of all that we understand as a person ; it may involve our integration into harmonies of which we are unaware so long as we are clogged with the passions of this earth.

> There's not the smallest orb which thou behold'st
> But in his motion like an angel sings,
> Still quiring to the young-eyed cherubins ;
> Such harmony is in immortal souls,
> But while this muddy vesture of decay
> Doth grossly close it in, we cannot hear it.

Whether some conscious part in that immortal destiny shall be ours, or whether we shall be, personally, extinguished as sparks whose purpose was served by their transient falling through a summer night, I do not know. I know that here and now is the struggle to manifest the love of God in love of the brethren. " It doth not yet appear what we shall be."

*   *   *

This book, which was begun in November, is drawing to its close in April. Beyond my window is the blue arch of the morning and the reflections of green trees undulating in water. The birds are in full song and the trees in full flower. Never have I known a lovelier spring. On plum and pear and apple the blossom is so thick, so busy with the fertilising toil of bees, that one would imagine nature was crying aloud to man, her thus-far idiot child, to take note of the beauty of constructive work in this his world of destruction. The *abundance* of the scene is almost overbearing; and it is through this abundant world that men are blasting and hacking their way, pouring down fire from the skies upon earth and sea alike. The fishermen tell me that they draw in their nets full of dead fish, and the fish, no doubt, feed fat on dead men. Death everywhere on this morning that cries aloud : " I am come that ye might have life, and that ye might have it more abundantly."

Always man tells himself that there is a spiritual excuse for his descent into barbarism. He must have his God of Battles. More than a hundred years ago, I learn from Mr. Jack Simmons's book *Southey*, the poet was writing of the war with Napoleon as " a business of natural life and death, a war of virtue against vice, light against darkness, the good principle against the evil one " ; and to-day, in Mr. Rom Landau's book *The Wing*, one finds the words echoed : " The issues at stake are so clear, and the spiritual character of the opposing forces in this war are so unequivocally defined. . . ."

What are the opposing forces ? It is not a matter of conjecture but of knowledge that before the war began a rich and influential section of opinion in England, France and America was favourably disposed to Hitler, even after the predatory nature of his designs was plain for all to see. "How much money can we lend him, at what interest ? " was the first question ; and the second

question : "What is he doing with this money ?" was not
even asked. That would be interfering with the rights of
a sovereign state. It is equally a matter of knowledge that
in those countries the same section of opinion was—and in
England and America to a large extent still is—suspicious
of Russia's direction and intention. In the actual *débâcle*
that is now upon us, the "opposing forces", for reasons of
temporary expediency, have become rather complicated
and difficult to disentangle. There has been some reason
to doubt, for example, whether the Greeks, ranged with
our side of the "opposing forces", are without dilution
ministers of God's grace. All we can say with certainty
is that the failure of love in the world has involved men in
one of their recurring tragedies and that the breakdown of
inhibitions which this has caused has revealed the Germans
as a peculiarly bestial and abandoned race, horrifying and
obnoxious to the sane sentiments of humanity. It has,
furthermore, shown man's mechanical ingenuity to be
advanced so far beyond his moral stature—nature's idiot-
child having the brow of Prospero as façade to the soul of
Caliban—that he is, for the moment, in a state of panic
at the consequences of his own doings. The fullness of
these consequences does not yet appear, but will do so.
He will yet have further cause to know that one does not
pull down half the world, demolish the great traditional
monuments of human history, and then automatically step
into paradise. The years ahead withhold their secrets, but
they will be governed, like all else, by the law of cause

and effect. What effects may be expected to follow the causes we see about us, let each man deduce for himself. For me, I should put disillusion, toil and poverty high among them. There is a glib phrase about the "economics of plenty". Well, we shall see.

This bestiality of the Germans to which I have referred is now so well established a fact that I for one could do with less writing about it in the newspapers. It is desirable, even necessary, that we should know about these things. Well, now we *do* know, and the continued repetition of identical detail can be spared us. I say this not out of squeamishness but because I think the continued publication of these loathsome details may well help in the corruption of young minds already assaulted by the "gangster" films of the cinemas and the newspaper pictures of death and destruction as the normal expression of living. The war has now lasted so long that there is a whole young generation which is entering its second decade with no knowledge of anything else. It is a generation in which problems of what are called "delinquency" are beginning to appear. Is it to be wondered at that children take to smashing windows when there is held up before their notice as admirable the smashing of whole cities? Is it surprising that they should kill a calf when the "liquidation" of thousands of men is an occurrence daily reported ? Many of them know nothing of the daily rhythm of normal life : the father going forth to his work in the morning and returning in the evening, thus establishing in the young mind the connection between life and labour. "Child delinquents", anyway, is a phrase to make angels laugh as they contemplate on the one hand these cheeky young apple-stealers and on the other the word of condemnation issuing from the mouth of a generation that is wrecking the loveliest things man has made.

The object of publishing "torture" stories is to make us hate the Germans, whereas what we should in fact learn to hate is the police state wheresoever it exists. This does not alter the fact that humanity must take note and take action concerning this unprecedented uprush of the filthiest sediment of the human mind. I suggest that the appropriate action would be the compiling of a book by a competent authority dealing with all the episodes of horror and torture that have been established beyond a doubt, and that, to put the matter outside conjecture, every episode should be confessed to, in the pages of a book, by a German who knew the facts. This black book of infamy, with a preface in which any civilised government that cared to do so expressed its horror and contempt of German method, should then take the place of *Mein Kampf* as compulsory reading in German schools. Not among infants, but in the senior classes. The indelible disgust which the German record has impressed in the hearts of more civilised men could be emphasised by an examination on the book's contents. This might—who knows?—do some good; but, for us, we have had enough of torture stories. I have read novels about this war containing the most revolting and minute descriptions of long-drawn-out physical tortures. No one ever suggests that they should be " banned ". Only novels dealing with the affairs of sex, which are creative, are banned. Torture, which is destructive, seems from this point of view to worry nobody. It is not in the category of "immorality". I imagine that these torture novels would get by the censors even in Southern Ireland, so holy a place that no novel may suggest within its chaste frontiers that any child is begotten save by a ghost, holy or otherwise, or born of anything but a virgin or a mulberry bush.

* * *

When I began to write this book, my intention was to put into it such thoughts and observations as visited me day by day. It has turned out differently from my expectations. Comment upon a letter written to a newspaper led to the reflection that war is a consequence of the undeveloped moral nature of man. On the plane of physical hardihood, of meeting with such resolution as we may the blows that fate (which means man's antecedent conduct) rains upon us : on that plane Mr. Churchill might rightly speak of " our finest hour ". But a morally awakened race, living the life of love which is the life of harmony with God's purpose, may well look back upon these years as the years of mankind's deepest degradation. Unless, that is, another, even finer, hour is before us.

These things being so, it was borne increasingly upon

my mind that now, in the midst of the tumult, we must seek for its fatal and destructive causes, because the one fact that becomes clear is that war is not achieving the only thing that could be its justification : that is, redemption from war. Even at this late hour of the present conflict, the threat of future war hangs over us with angry menace. Man, rushing into war, has shouted " Never again ! " too often for the words to deceive a child. It is clear that war will cease only when men refuse any longer to wage it, when " Never again ! " means " This time ", not " Next time ". It is clear also that, with the increasing regimentation of national policies, the deepening shadow of the state's hand upon all human activity, this renunciation of war as a weapon will never be made by a state. It is a matter for individual decision.

In examining this view, I was led into a consideration of the place of religion in the individual life, which is the only place where it can be fruitful. And since such a consideration would be a mere academic excursion if conducted " in general ", I found myself engaged in an assessment of my own religious beliefs. It was here that the book went wrong, or right, according as the reader may decide. In the beginning, I had no intention of unveiling my own intimacies, and now at the end I hesitate to do so. Religion, unlike theology, is something to be lived rather than talked or written about ; and my position in any case is, I am aware, too full of contradictions, too experimental, to be of value to anyone but myself.

My profoundest and most insoluble contradiction lies

in my attitude to war itself, and I might as well face it
in all its baffling mystery. While I am convinced, with an
unshakable conviction, that war will never be banished by
any national or international pacts, agreements, outlawings,
or what you like, but only by the slow and tedious growth
of pacifist belief and practice in individual lives, with some
world-wide organisation such as the Christian church for
its point of accretion, nevertheless I am not myself a good
enough man to give my own adherence to the venture.
I am trapped in the human dilemma which is caused by the
unequal growth of moral consciousness. I do not believe,
as Southey believed of the Napoleonic war and as Mr.
Rom Landau believes of this one, that we are fighting on
the side of light against darkness; only that our gloom is
less profound than the satanic cloud in which pain and
torture are arrayed. "Lighten our darkness" should be
our cry, as theirs; but because our darkness is shot through
by a little gleam, and because we fear to lose this spark
through the victory of a greater darkness, we rush into the
impossible breach. Above all things, the dilemma of the
human heart is its generous impulse to be present—even
if it can do little—when the trumpet sounds and the thick
arrows fall. Little indeed. In the last war, physical frailty
permitted me none but an ignoble part; in this, I have
served in the Home Guard. To this ludicrous extent, I
have twice voluntarily enlisted, and I should still, so con-
tradictory is my nature, feel shame to be a "pressed man".
A psychologist would tell me that obedience to the herd
instinct had twice taken me within the warm and com-

fortable embrace of a prevailing opinion ; but I think there is more in it than that. And this something more is the deep human feeling for one's kind in its hour of adversity, a desire to stand by and help to bear the blows, whether deserved or undeserved, whether the consequences of our own sins and follies or not. This profound emotion that goes out from man to man when the cloud of calamity bursts is the greatest obstacle that the pacifist has to surmount, and one that I find insurmountable. The man who is great enough to surmount it must *appear* to be lacking in love for his fellows, because his love for *all* his fellows, his enemies as well as his kin, overbears the expedient love of those immediately about him, even when these have a cause that is, measured by our temporal standards, a finer one than that which opposes them. The salt of the earth who can attain to that love, which is denied to me (save in its admiration) will understand the position of Jesus when, turning to his mother, he asked : " Woman, what have I to do with thee ? " It was not that his love for her was the less, but that the concerns of all mankind called for his dedication. And still they are calling.

*   *   *

For many years I have not attended Church, and the reason is that I could not honestly repeat the Creed. The Creed I could repeat would run something like this : I believe in God the Father Almighty, Maker of heaven and earth, and in Jesus who revealed that the Father's almightiness is the almightiness of love. I believe in the Holy Spirit, the Communion of Loving Men, the forgiveness of sins, and the perpetuation of earthly life in life everlasting. Amen.

But do I need a creed ? Does it matter *what* I believe ? The question is being increasingly asked, and, of course, creeds don't matter if they are only what you say you believe, or what, indeed, you may think you believe. They matter only if they are what you believe and if " knowing these things, ye do them ".

The cause of the contemporary tragedy is a moral and not a physical cause, which is to say that it is bound up with creeds. There is a widespread and mistaken belief that all we have to do to put things right is to arrange for a better distribution of the world's goods. We have done well enough with production, the economists tell us, but we haven't been so good at distribution. But when you have done all that—if ever you do it—and it is a matter of elementary decency that it should be done—you will still be faced by the truth that you do not necessarily produce a better man by producing a better-fed and better-housed man. You can satisfy all the physical needs of all the world and be as far from a morally mature world as ever. You could still have a world of people who did not mature but merely grew adult, seeking more and more nothing but the grown-up version of the toys of their infancy. In such a world disaster is inherent.

254

Though both England and America have a long way
to go before even the physical needs of their people are
met as fully as they should be, it is yet true that a poor
man in the West enjoys a condition of physical well-being
that would seem riches to the workers of the East. Commenting on this, Mr. John Goette, who was for many years
a newspaper reporter in Japan, says in *Japan Fights for
Asia* : " We come upon the paradox that Japan went to
war against the United States because she admired us and
the American way of life. . . . It is the dream of practically every Japanese to enjoy a life as nearly American as
he can make it. They like our jazz, our dance-halls, our
movies, our hot-dogs, our ice-cream sodas, and our flashing electric-light signs. They copy our skyscrapers, our
hotels and our trains. They wear our clothes . . ." and
so on through a long catalogue down to the conclusion :
" If a modern Japanese can indulge himself in all the *outward* attributes of American living, he is at once satisfied
and proud."

Leave that aside for a moment and consider some extracts from another book, dealing with another Eastern
race : Mr. James Burke's *My Father in China*. This is
the story of William Burke, an American, who spent the
whole of his long life as a missionary to the Chinese.
Burke's first sermon, his son tells us, ended with these
words : " In the country of the Flowery Flag, where I
come from, everyone worships Zaung Ti and His Son.
Because of that, there is no misery or sin in that country."

255

Soon after this, Burke was transferred from a rural district to Shanghai, and his son writes : " Shanghai was no haven of virtue before the Boxer crisis, and the new sediment of adventurers, gamblers and camp followers settling there in the wake of the foreign troops took nothing away from its celebrated tourist name, Paris of the Far East. Heavy drinking was proverbial ; gambling a major industry ; opium a legitimate business ; prostitutes a hallowed institution. As these plain facts pressed into Burke's once-serene conscience, his sermons to the Chinese began losing their references to the West, particularly America, as the embodiment of Christian culture."

It is hardly surprising to read that, after forty-one years of work in the country, Burke said : " The Chinese are difficult subjects to convert to Christianity at best. They are satisfied with the religion they have."

I marked with italics what seemed to me the significant word in the passage from Mr. Goette's book : " If a modern Japanese can indulge himself in all the *outward* attributes of American living, he is at once satisfied and proud." If the East is uninterested in the *inward* attributes of Western civilisation—in freedom and justice and love— then the West must ask itself why its advocacy of such things in the East has been less striking and attractive than its advocacy of slick and easy living. And the answer is that these things seemed more attractive to the East because they were more attractive to us. We infect others by what is most potent in ourselves. Merely to repeat the creed of love, which is self-forgetfulness, is inoperative when all your actions are crying out that your deepest belief is in self-indulgence.

And as it has been in the relationship of East and West, so it has been in the relationship everywhere of the more morally-awakened nations with others. We have not wanted war, but have we so passionately advocated and exemplified the spirit of love, which is war's negation, that from this an infection of good might spread ? In short, what is our creed—really, not professedly ? This is the question that underlies not only our present dilemma but all the future of the human race. To give men bread is excellent and necessary, but the establishment of the kingdom of love will not flow from it. But *it* will flow from the establishment of the kingdom of love. Humanity will never know peace till the thing is seen the right way round. The promise is not : Seek all these things and the Kingdom of God shall be added unto you ; but : Seek ye *first* the Kingdom of God and His righteousness, and all these things shall be added unto you.

The validity of this saying appears in the fact that the world is now demonstrably putting it the wrong way round with the dire and catastrophic effects that follow the violation of a law of the universe ; and also in the fact that innumerable private lives have proved that the law works, down to the last detail of its promise, when put the right way round. And the detail of the promise is not that those who seek to be good citizens of the kingdom of

257

love shall have all that they want of earthly things. The promise is not that they shall have all that they want; but all that they need. And it is in the nature of their new citizenship that they shall need but little of the things of the world. They may have them—even abundantly; but they will know that they do not need them and thus they will be unconcerned about their loss. We could all be much poorer than we are and bear it well enough. Loss is not disaster. Disaster is in the constant cancerous *fear* of loss. When had we less than in June 1940? When were we so lifted up, so without fear, as then when nothing but our naked breasts were opposed to the mightiest machine the world has known?

Henry Drummond wrote a book called *Natural Law in the Spiritual World*. "Seek ye first the Kingdom" would appear to be also a spiritual law in the natural world. It is a saying that I have pondered over for many hours during many months. I can detect no flaw in its application, find no instance of its failing to "work". It is the master-saying of all spiritual revelation. It has no truck with "non-attachment" but recognises man's physical as well as spiritual need and tells him how both may be satisfied. It is the key-word that the world is seeking, the identification of those things that belong unto our peace.

MYLOR:

> *November 1, 1944*
> *April 19, 1945*

EPILOGUE

THE writing of this book ended in April. It is now mid-August, and in the meantime a lot has happened in the world. I shall not say that victory, much less peace, has been achieved in Europe, but at any rate physical fighting has ended there, and the prostrate continent begins to give off the effluvia of epidemic, starvation and neurosis. All sorts of odours are drifting towards us—except the fragrance of peace.

The war against Japan has ended, too. I do not find it remarkable that a sense of joy at this fulfilment is lacking. Mr. Richard Strout, the special correspondent in Washington of *The Sunday Times*, wrote the other day : " Though America widely believes that the Pacific war is over, or all but over . . . thoughtful people already display a curious new sense of insecurity, hardly in keeping with what seems to be the victorious end of the great war era."

This new sense of insecurity seems to me to be anything but " curious ". The atomic bomb has admitted a new terror into the relationships of men, and the course of scientific events has made it possible for this terror to reach America as easily as any other part of the globe. The century which England enjoyed, when wars were remote and their horrors unthinkable as far as experience within the island went, that century which 1940 hustled into the halcyon of the past, was marked by a delicious complacent sense of untouchability ; and this sense, which we then enjoyed, America, even up to a week ago, seems to have imagined was as much her inalienable birthright as life, liberty and the pursuit of happiness. The most childish American can no longer live in this fool's paradise : hence the " curious new sense of insecurity ".

Thus the " global " war has drawn to its close with the words " victory " and " defeat " more meaningless than ever, with nothing achieved but loss, nothing created but new problems of a magnitude and complexity that must engender widespread friction and frustration ; and, above all, with the atomic bomb asking its enigmatic question : Little man, what now ?

The primary thing to note about the discovery of the atomic bomb is that it is a discovery within the region of the material. It does nothing that man has not been able to do for untold centuries, but it does it more terribly and extensively. Already there are enthusiasts who tell us that by atomic-power propulsion we shall be able to reach the planets. Well, what of that ? What shall we find there save a world of matter like our own ?

Others tell us that by this means we shall solve the problem of giving men all the food and clothes, the heat and light, that they need. But we could have done this at any time during the last hundred years, if we had wanted to. The world already is full to overflowing with all that man needs and with the means to make this accessible to all

260

men. Nothing has lacked save the religious sense of brotherhood which would have seen that the thing was done; and this new extension of merely physical power cannot, because of its material nature, supply that. All that has happened is that we have taken an enormous physical step forward, with no corresponding step on the spiritual plane; and thereby we have enlarged the already dangerous dissonance and disparity between knowledge and wisdom.

The scientists tell us that we shall not, in any case, see the application of atomic power to daily life—(merely to occasional death)—for a long time to come. But suppose that the marvels of the new atomic era were to reach fruition to-morrow. What then? The world thus conditioned would be lived in by you—you who read these words. Try not to think of the glorious emancipated beings of scientific-romantic invention. Think of yourself, as you know yourself to be. Would your essential needs and aspirations be different from what they are to-day? You would require food, clothing and shelter, and these you have. (If the world lived by its religious sense, all men would have them.) If your clothing is of spun glass instead of wool or cotton; if your food is prepared by a chemical formula and hygienically tinned instead of being cooked in a kitchen; if your house is of some new plastic material instead of brick or stone or wood: What of all this? You are still you. All this increase of physical power will perhaps have given you more leisure;

261

but, of its nature, this being physical, it can give you nothing with which that leisure may be filled. And, for what the observation may be worth, it is a fact that the most empty-headed and empty-hearted people I know in the world as it is are those who have most leisure. All *that* part of the matter will continue to depend on what we call interior resource ; and though in material conditions your life may seem to be different—though, in fact, the difference will be of appearance only—here, in the realm of the heart and the spirit, you will find that nothing has changed at all ; and it is these invisible elements of life that are eternal, and the rest ephemeral. All the phenomena of the " atomic age ", assuming mankind does not destroy itself in producing it, will pass away at last into the romantic limbo of done-with things, like medieval castles and the slums of Victorian England, and, in whatever world may follow that, the thirsty soul of man will still pant for living water.

A point of immediate practical interest and importance bears upon the widespread belief that these are " democratic " days. " Democracy " and " Christendom " are words which I find myself examining with closer and closer attention whenever I come upon them. They are booby-traps of political and religious expression. This atomic bomb was produced out of the scientific skill and the financial wealth of England and America, the two outstanding " democracies " of our time. It is profitable to spare a moment to watch " democracy " at work on this matter. Mr. Truman, the American President, in his statement to the world, says this : "We have now two great plants and many lesser works devoted to the production of atomic power. Employment during peak construction numbered 125,000, and over 65,000 individuals are even now engaged in operating the plants. Many have worked there for two and a half years. *Few know what they have been producing.* They see great quantities of material going in, and *they see nothing coming out.*"

So we see "democracy", under the command of a handful of scientific supermen, blindly labouring to pull out of the bottle the cork which has now released the genius who can never be put back. "They didn't know what they were doing and they saw nothing." That is how democracy works to-day.

Of course, I shall be told, this was inevitable. We were not alone in our search for the secret of atomic energy. The Germans were after it, too. We could not shout from the house-tops what we were doing.

That is true. A nation embarked upon warfare in this scientific age cannot draw back before even the most dreadful implications. Once it is in up to the knees, there remains nothing but Macbeth's fatal cry :

> I am in blood
> Stepp'd in so far, that should I wade no more,
> Returning were as tedious as go o'er.

263

What I am here concerned with is not to inquire
whether it is necessary to keep " democracy " in the dark,
but to stress that; in fact, " Democracy " *is* being kept in
the dark about matters which may involve the whole
future of man on the planet. It may indeed be wondered
whether this word, once of a great and heartening consequence, has not fallen into idiocy and contempt in a world
which, whether " democracy " cares to acknowledge it or
not, is increasingly swayed by a few hands on the master-
keys.

Much, then, I say, has happened since this book was
written ; but nothing, I think, to make me qualify the
fundamental contention of one section of it. That contention is that force will not, in the long run, profit man
in his living on this earth. That we have now force in
its greatest conceivable manifestation, " harnessing ", as
Mr. Truman proudly says, " the basic power of the universe ", does not alter my argument one whit. If I am
right, Mr. Truman is wrong ; for I believe that the basic
power of the universe is not force, but love. Mr. Truman
is talking of the material universe ; but that is not all that
is to be said of the matter.

Force is force, and it is my argument that the stone
with which Cain battered in Abel's head and the atomic
bomb that has now fallen on Hiroshima are in the same
moral category. Morally, from the moment of Abel's
murder to the disruption of Hiroshima, we have stood still,
and to announce that we are now able to use " the force

264

from which the sun draws its power " does nothing but darken the brand that God puts upon our brow, for of us it cannot be said, " They know not what they do."

The scientific pluto-democracy, which I find the best description of the western world to-day, is not noticeably increasing our ration of love ; but, also, it can do nothing —literally nothing—to separate us from our love and from our God. If I did not believe this, I should fear the world I live in, and I do not see how, to any man who has not access to God's love, the world of to-day and to-morrow can be anything but a nightmare.

There is only one conclusion in this book which later thought would make me wish to alter. On page 49 I say that it is a matter of simple observation that the British and American people are in a higher state of moral development than the Germans. Now that the bomb has been dropped on Hiroshima, I would not defend this opinion with much heat.

August 15, 1945.

HOWARD SPRING author of *And Another Thing . . .*

Howard Spring was born in Cardiff, South Wales, in 1889 where he spent the first twenty-two years of his life. His father, an Irishman, was a gardener. He died when Spring was twelve years old, leaving a wife and seven children. The mother took washing and mangling into the home and went out charing. Young Howard left school to take a series of temporary jobs as errand boy for a grocer and butcher and worked for a time as an office boy for a wage of less than a dollar a week. When he was thirteen he became a messenger for the *South Wales Daily News* and by the time he left this paper, at the age of twenty-two, he was a full-fledged reporter. He subsequently reported for the *Yorkshire Observer* and the *Manchester Guardian*.

Mr. Spring served in the British Army during the First World War and was attached to Army Intelligence. After the war he returned to the *Manchester Guardian* and was assigned to write on the troubles in Ireland. Here he gained a knowledge and understanding of the Irish problem which was to be revealed in his novel, *My Son, My Son!* At the age of forty-three Mr. Spring left the *Manchester Guardian* to become literary critic of the London *Evening Standard*. During the Second World War he served in the Cornwall Home Guard. He accompanied Mr. Churchill on the occasion of the signing of the Atlantic Charter. His two sons both served in the Royal Navy during the war.